PRAISE FOR
Heart of an Athlete™

Athletics can be a great way to learn lessons about everyday life. But what is really special is when you can take athletic lessons and apply them to your spiritual life. *Heart of an Athlete* takes a look at how the tests we face as players and coaches can help us grow as Christians.

COACH TONY DUNGY
Head Coach, Indianapolis Colts

Staying close to God through the study of His Word is an essential part of any Christian's life. The devotions in *Heart of an Athlete* will help you dig into the Word and be encouraged not only in your faith but also in your sport.

BETSY KING
Member, LPGA Tour Hall of Fame

Heart of an Athlete is a training manual with an eternal goal. Being an athlete, I realize the importance of training and preparing my body so that it is ready for competition. This book will help you train so that you can live life the way God intended.

CHRIS KLEIN
Midfielder, Kansas City Wizards

HEART
OF AN
ATHLETE™

Revell

a division of Baker Publishing Group
Grand Rapids, Michigan

Published by Revell
a division of Baker Publishing Group
PO Box 6287, Grand Rapids, MI 49516-6287
www.revellbooks.com

Revell edition published 2014
ISBN 978-0-8007-2505-1

Previously published by Regal Books

Printed in the United States of America

The Library of Congress has cataloged the previous edition as follows:
    Heart of an athlete / Fellowship of Christian Athletes.
       p. cm.
    ISBN 0-8307-3850-9 (trade paper)
    1. Athletes—Prayer-books and devotions—English. I. Fellowship of Christian Athletes
    BV4596.A8H33 2005
    242'.68—dc22   2005028778

15 16 17 18 19 20 21   8 7 6 5 4 3 2

Contents

Foreword

Becoming Authentic Men and Women of God

Too many of today's athletes are just out for themselves. I see it in the National Football League and I am sure that you see it in your sport and league. Selfishness is rampant. Players make their sport their god. I know, because there was a time when I did it, too.

When I was younger, football was my world. I was successful in high school and in college. I was one of the best kickers around and was drafted by the New York Giants. I was injured during my first season but celebrated as my team won the Super Bowl. It couldn't get any better, or so it seemed. A few years later I found myself struggling. Football was supposed to bring so much joy, but it was killing me. The pressure was immense. After missing a 19-yard field goal, I cried out, "Lord, help me!" right there on the field. Before that day, I had always known of God but did not have a relationship with Him.

It took a little more time, but I finally got to the point where I realized that I had to surrender my football career to God. I had to let go. I heard someone talk about Mark 8:35-36: "For whoever wants to save his life will lose it, but whoever loses his life because of Me and the gospel will save it. For what does it benefit a man to gain the whole world yet lose his life?" For me, that verse contained the answer. Looking back, I can see that God had a plan all along. I had to get to the point of seeing that it was not about me; it was about Him.

As I write this foreword, I am in the middle of my sixteenth season of professional football. I now play for the Baltimore Ravens. In these 16 years, I have seen a lot of success, including another Super Bowl championship and being named to the Pro Bowl team. God has placed me here and given me this platform. It is a gift to be able to speak to young players and to be able to write to you now.

When I speak at FCA camps and other places, I talk about taking personal responsibility as Christians. There are many big issues in our lives. Money, pride in physical ability, and the availability of sex can deceive us as athletes. The world tells us that these will satisfy us, that they are *it*. I can tell you, I have had *it* and got *it*, and *it* is not it.

True satisfaction only comes when we have a relationship with God, accept our responsibilities as authentic men and women of God, and put others before ourselves. One of the best ways to do this is to have a daily devotional time. It is pretty simple: Talk with God and read His Word—the Bible. That's what this book of devotional readings is all about. Just take a few minutes each day to connect with God. These readings, written by athletes like you and me, will help you get started. As you read, let go of yourself and allow Jesus Christ to take control.

Matt Stover
Kicker
Baltimore Ravens

Teammate:

For over 50 years, FCA has been privileged to minister to athletes and coaches by encouraging and equipping them to know and serve the master coach, Jesus Christ. One of our priorities is to develop resources to engage athletes and help them integrate their faith and sport.

Being on a team is all about relationships. Whether it's a fellow teammate, a friend or a member of our family, the only way to get to know a person is to spend time with him or her. These 90 devotionals are designed to help you develop a focused time with God. They are written from a competitor's point of view and include key verses from the Bible to help you gain an understanding of God's perspective on issues that you face in your daily life. Our hope is that this book will motivate you to have a consistent training time and read God's Playbook to deepen your understanding of His Word.

As an athlete, you have been given a tremendous platform to influence others. Our prayer is that God will use these devotions to transform your life as a competitor so that you can make an eternal impact, not only in your life, but also in the lives of others.

God Speed,

Les Steckel

Les Steckel
FCA President/CEO

Training Time

In sports and in life, there is always the need to take a time-out to think about your purpose in living and playing for God. FCA is excited to present you with a collection of devotions that will challenge you to play and live for the glory of God. Each devotion is written from the athletic perspective and will encourage you to be more like Christ both on and off the field.

Every morning, set aside a special quiet time or spiritual training time to be with God. During this time, talk to God and let Him speak to you through the Bible. There are many effective methods that can be used for your daily time with God. One method that we recommend is the following PRESS method.

The PRESS Method

Pray

Begin your quiet time by thanking God for the new day, and then ask Him to help you learn from what you read. Prepare yourself by

- · clearing your mind and being quiet before the Lord
- · asking God to settle your heart
- · listening to worship music to prepare your spirit
- · asking God to give you a teachable heart

Read

Begin with the 90 devotionals provided in this book. Also, try reading a chapter of Proverbs every day (there are 31 chapters in Proverbs, which makes it ideal for daily reading), one psalm and/or a chapter out of the Old or New Testament. You may consider beginning with one of the Gospels (Matthew, Mark, Luke or John), or one of the shorter letters such as Ephesians or James.

Examine

Ask yourself the following questions in regard to the passage you read:

- *Teaching:* What do I need to *know* about God, myself and others?
- *Rebuking:* What do I need to *stop* doing—sins, habits, selfish patterns?
- *Correcting:* What do I need to *change* in my thoughts, attitudes or actions?
- *Training:* What do I need to *do* in obedience to God's leading?

Summarize

Do one of the following:

- Discover what the passage reveals about God and His character, what it says or promises about you, and what it says or promises about others (such as your parents, friends or teammates). Write your thoughts down in a personal journal.
- Rewrite one or two key verses in your own words.
- Outline what each verse is saying.
- Give each verse a one-word title that summarizes what it says.

Share

Talk with God about what you've learned. Also, take time each day to share with someone what you learned during that day's study. Having a daily training time is the key to spiritual development. If you commit to working through these 90 devotionals over the next three months, you will establish this as a habit—one that will be vital to your growth in Christ.

If you are committed to establishing this daily training time with God, fill out the box below.

I will commit to establishing this daily habit.

Signed _____ Today's Date _____

Writers

We have assembled athletes, coaches and team chaplains from all levels (in addition to FCA staff) to contribute their time, talent and experience in writing these devotions. These writers come from diverse backgrounds and include representatives from a variety of sports, including baseball, soccer, basketball, football, lacrosse, track and field, and others. You can check out each of these writers' minibiographies in the contributors section at the end of the book.

Format

Ready   A verse or passage from Scripture that focuses or directs your heart and mind. Turn to the scripture reference in your Bible and read it within the overall context of the passage.

Set   A teaching point (a story, training point or thought taken from a sports perspective) that draws a lesson from the passage.

Go   Questions that will help you examine your heart and challenge you to apply God's truth to your life—on and off the field.

Workout   Additional scripture references to help you dig deeper.

Overtime   A closing prayer that will help you commit to the Lord what you have learned.

To receive the daily e-mail devotional
"FCA's Impact Play," go to www.FCA.org.

Ready

So if anyone purifies himself from these things, he will be a special instrument, set apart, useful to the Master, prepared for every good work.

2 TIMOTHY 2:21

Set

Since 1997, MasterCard has received hundreds of awards for their catchy ad campaign featuring the slogan "Priceless." As Christians, I think the slogan for our relationships with Christ should be "Serving Is Priceless." Most people think that *serving* is the same thing as *service*. I disagree. I believe there is a huge difference between the two. Christ did not come to give good service; He came to serve. As an athlete, I am not supposed to give good service to my teammates— I am to serve them. As a coach, I serve my team; I do not provide them a service. Service is something you pay for or something you expect, such as courteous and prompt attention from the employees at a restaurant or gas station. But serving goes deeper. Serving deals with heart issues and involves sacrifice and meeting real needs.

Christ desires that we as athletes and coaches become servants to our teammates, friends, family and communities. He has set us apart for a great work. We are His instruments—His serving instruments! Today, this can be a hard concept to understand. It seems like everyone in the world of sports wants to be a leader, not a servant. Jesus never told us to be leaders, but He did tell us to be servants.

This summer, FCA had more than 7,000 athletes attend FCA Leadership Camps. At one of the camps, I shared with the students that they were really at a Servant Camp, not a Leadership Camp. To be a leader you must serve, and this is my challenge to you today. Fulfill Christ's calling on your life and become a servant!—*Dan Britton*

Go

1. On a scale of 1 to 5, how well are you serving others (teammates, coaches, friends, family)?

2. Do you give service when Christ wants you to engage in serving? If so, when?
3. How has God gifted you to serve? How has He set you apart? Are you using your ability to serve?

Workout
Ephesians 2:10; 2 Timothy 2:14-21

Overtime
Lord, teach me how to serve. My teammates and friends need to see what Jesus looks like. I pray that when I serve they will be able to see You. Help me to fully understand that You have set me apart for a great work. Amen.

Play the B.U.G.

Ready
A truthful witness gives honest testimony, but a false witness tells lies. Reckless words pierce like a sword, but the tongue of the wise brings healing. Truthful lips endure forever, but a lying tongue lasts only a moment.
PROVERBS 12:17-19, *NIV*

Set
Even as the words float off the end of my tongue, I realize that I have blown it. This kind of situation usually involves me saying negative words to my teammates or others. It's so easy for me to become the "cut-down king." It doesn't take much, and it could involve something as simple as calling someone a name.

You know the routine: You cut one of your teammates down, and your other teammates laugh. You may try to justify your unkind remarks with the fact that everyone does it, but the truth is that those reckless words cut. They pierce like a sword and cause damage.

Instead of playing the Cut Down game in which we just "go with the flow" and cut others down because everyone else is doing it, God desires us to play the B.U.G., or the Build Up Game. This game takes effort, and we have to be intentional to play. It doesn't come naturally, either. But when it's played, it is awesome.

The B.U.G. blesses so many people. A friend of mine once said that everyone in the world is underencouraged, and I agree! I ask the Lord to show me ways that I can encourage teammates, friends, family members and even people I don't know. I want to build others up and show love through my words.

I believe that the tongue can heal. Are you ready to play the B.U.G.? —*Dan Britton*

Go

1. Why is it so difficult to build others up? What is in your heart that prevents you from blessing others with your tongue?
2. Do you believe your words can heal? Has anyone ever healed you with his or her words?
3. What is one way that you can play the B.U.G. on your team? With your coaches?

Workout
Psalm 15:2; Proverbs 16:21; Colossians 3:16

Overtime
Lord, I play the Cut Down game way too often. Today, I desire to start playing the B.U.G. Teach me ways to build others up so that I can be a blessing. May my words heal, not damage— may they lift others up and not pull them down. I know people in my life who need to receive a word of encouragement. I pray for opportunities to bring life with my words. Amen.

Constructive Criticism

An ear that listens to life-giving rebukes will be at home among the wise. Anyone who ignores instruction despises himself, but whoever listens to correction acquires good sense.

PROVERBS 15:31-32

Set

One of a coach's toughest jobs is telling athletes what they are doing wrong. Most coaches try to do it constructively, but even then many athletes will choose to ignore the instruction or make excuses, blaming everyone else for the problems *they themselves* have caused.

Recently, I, too, was reminded of my imperfection through constructive criticism. What a blow to my ego that was! But we all need correction and people who will speak truth into our lives. Although we do not always want to hear what they are telling us, we still get to choose how we respond to the correction. Many of us choose to take criticism personally, and that holds us back from making the necessary changes for the better. Those of us who can listen to this type of correction and react accordingly will no doubt be better off in the end.

I have seen far too many athletes handle constructive criticism poorly, and it has ruined many a good athletic career. I myself would have to plead guilty to not always taking criticism the right way. But Christ wants to speak truth into our lives, many times in the form of the Holy Spirit's constructive criticism. Again, we have a choice to respond positively or make it personal. The Lord knows that this criticism is for our own good, and when we realize that, our relationship with Him will deepen.

We need to remember that most people who offer constructive criticism truly are trying to help us. Words of encouragement should prod us on to a greater life in Christ, not lead to the bitterness of spirit that brings glory to Satan and his troops. So the next time someone gives you constructive criticism, just say, "Thanks for caring enough to tell me what was on your heart." —*Jere Johnson*

1. How do you handle constructive criticism?
2. Do you try to make yourself feel better by finding fault in the messenger?
3. How can you respond properly to constructive criticism?

Workout
Proverbs 10:17; 12:1; 15; Hebrews 12:4-11

Overtime
God, I know that I need to be open to instruction from my coaches if I am going to be a successful athlete. I don't want to be limited by my pride. Adjust my attitude and help me as I work to receive instruction with an open heart. Amen.

One Way 2 Play

Ready
Be strong and very courageous. Be careful to obey all the law my servant Moses gave you; do not turn from it to the right or to the left, that you may be successful wherever you go.
JOSHUA 1:7, *NIV*

Set
Most students who find themselves in situations or places that they hoped they'd never be do so because of tiny compromises that they made early in their life journey. I have never met a student who has ever identified alcoholism as a career goal. Neither have I met an ambitious student whose "Top 10 Things to Do Before Graduation" included becoming a parent prematurely, getting kicked off the team, or losing the trust and respect of their parents.

Although most students would want to avoid these misfortunes like the plague, many engage in behaviors that increase the probability of them experiencing these situations. These compromises are common among all teens, black or white, rich or poor, and regardless of whether they live in the city or suburbs.

Almost always, the common denominator is drug use. It doesn't matter if it's a cigarette here or there, an occasional beer or hard liquor drink, or weed, blunts, ecstasy or heroin. Drugs will always diminish the masterpiece that is you! You are a miracle of God. When you are high or enhanced, the end result of what you've smoked, drunk, popped or huffed will always be defeat.

Most of those who compromise do so because of the absence of three things: *faith in Christ, commitment* and *accountability*. I am so glad that when I was a teen, I had *faith* enough to believe that if I did what was right, all the right things in life would come back to me. I'm glad I had the courage and strength to *commit* to being drug-free and not turn to the left or right of that commitment. I'm also glad that I surrounded myself with like-minded people who held me *accountable* to my commitments. —*Steve Fitzhugh*

Go

1. What is your view on alcohol and drug use? Do you agree that using drugs will diminish the masterpiece that is you?
2. Are you compromising in the area of drug and alcohol use? If so, how?
3. What commitments will you make with regard to faith, commitment and accountability to be "one way 2 play"—drug and alcohol free?

Workout
Joshua 1:9; Psalm 84:11; 1 Corinthians 6:19; Hebrews 12:1-2

Overtime
God, help me as I make this commitment to remain drug free.
Help me identify an accountability partner—someone who
will help me to be faithful to my commitment and who will
ask me the tough questions each week. Amen.

Ready

Whether I come and see you or am absent, I will hear about you that you are standing firm in one spirit, with one mind, working side by side for the faith of the gospel, not being frightened in any way by your opponents.

PHILIPPIANS 1:27-28

Set

It happens all the time: As an athlete or coach, you are confronted with a situation in which your attitude will dictate your altitude. Someone does you wrong; a promise is broken; a ref makes a horrible call in a game; you are treated poorly. Whatever the circumstances, does your attitude show that God is in your life?

In his letter to the Philippians, Paul urged the believers to stand firm in their faith in Christ. Paul wanted everyone to stay focused on Christ and the glory of the cross, no matter what happened. In every situation we are under the authority of God, and we should act and react accordingly. Though we may be wronged, mistreated or severely tortured, we must stand firm, knowing that God will provide the victory.

Things happen in sports and in life. Teammates will fail you, coaches will misunderstand you, and officials will make unjust calls against you. But remember, how you respond will show others what is in your heart. Is your attitude above reproach? Can others tell that Christ is in you?

Respect all, fear none. That is God's calling for us. So face it—*it* happens to the best of us. Do your best through Christ to show that He truly rules in your life. —*Jere Johnson*

Go

1. Is your attitude flying high in Him, or is it way below His radar?
2. Are you submissive to those whom God has put in authority over you?

3. Today, how can you start to give total respect to those individuals whom the Lord has put in your life to lead you in your given situation?

Workout
Psalm 51; Philippians 1:20-30; James 1:2-6

Overtime
Lord, as I compete for You today, help me maintain an attitude that displays Your glory to all. May my mouth, my heart and my head be in total submission to You. Give me the strength to respect and honor those who do me wrong. Help me to serve You better today than I did yesterday. In the name of Jesus, I pray. Amen.

Team J.C.

Ready
Now the multitude of those who believed were of one heart and soul, and no one said that any of his possessions was his own, but instead they held everything in common. And with great power the apostles were giving testimony to the resurrection of the Lord Jesus, and great grace was on all of them.
ACTS 4:32-33

Set
NASCAR racing isn't necessarily thought of as a team sport by most people. But ask any driver and he will tell you that without a good pit crew, his chances of winning are slim.

Jeff Gordon credited his team for putting him in a position to win the 2005 Daytona 500, which he did by holding off Kurt Busch and Dale Earnhardt Jr. over the last two laps. "I knew over 500 miles, with that pit crew, that team, that hopefully some patience would ff there at the end."[1]

The FCA Competitor's Creed states that "I am a member of Team Jesus Christ." So what is it that constitutes membership on Jesus' team? I believe that we can learn some valuable insights from the Early Church in Acts. First of all, they had at their core the common bond of faith in Jesus Christ as His purposes. Second, they were obedient to Jesus' command to love one another sacrificially as He had loved them:

I give you a new commandment: that you love one another. Just as I have loved you, you should also love one another (John 13:34).

In sports, it is important that we have faith in our team and that everyone is on the same page regarding the team's goals and objectives. We must also be willing to give sacrificially of ourselves for the good of the team. Applying these principles will help us maximize the team's ultimate effectiveness. —*Josh Carter*

Go

1. What is the best team that you have ever been on? What were the key characteristics of this team?
2. How do these key characteristics apply to membership on Team Jesus Christ?
3. Are you a member of Team Jesus Christ? How do you know?

Workout
Luke 9:23; Acts 2:42-45; 1 John 3:14-23

Overtime
Lord, thank You for sacrificing Your Son and inviting me to be a member of Your team. I pray that You would help me have a sacrificial love for those on my team and those on Your team in a way that points people to You. Amen.

Ready

When the donkey saw the Angel of the Lord,
she crouched down under Balaam. So he became
furious and beat the donkey with his stick. Then the
Lord opened the donkey's mouth.

NUMBERS 22:27-28

Set

John was a great miler. He always liked to take the lead early in the race and run to victory. His coach, however, was concerned about an upcoming race. John's top opponent was a runner who liked to come from behind to win.

When the race started, John raced to the lead. His coach told him to move to the inside of lane one, but John ignored him. During laps two and three, his coach told him the same thing, but John again ignored him—he knew the victory was his. On lap four, John's coach became more insistent, but John stayed firm—and remained right in the middle of the lane.

On the final turn of the race, John's opponent passed him on the inside and took the victory. John's coach had seen what John himself had been blind to—that if John did not move to the inside, he would be beaten.

In the Old Testament, Balaam had a similar situation with his faithful donkey. Balaam was traveling down the road on his donkey when God became angry with him and sent an angel to oppose him. Three times the donkey avoided the angel, and each time Balaam became angry and hit his faithful steed. God had to open Balaam's eyes so that he could see the punishment that the donkey had saved him from. Only then did Balaam repent of his sin and turn to God for forgiveness.

John, like Balaam, had a blind spot and could not see what was coming. Many times, we do not listen to others who want to show us areas in which we can improve because we cannot see the need ourselves. But we need to pay attention to others. God may be using them to show us what we need to change today. —*Jere Johnson*

Go

1. What are the blind spots in your life?
2. Who has helped you see these blind spots?
3. How can you eliminate your spiritual blind spots?

Workout

Proverbs 12:15; 13:10; 15:22

Overtime

O Lord, please bring bold friends into my life—
true friends who can show me my spiritual blind spots.
Allow them to speak to me with truth in love. Amen.

I Was Wrong

Ready

Though a righteous man falls seven times, he will get up, but the wicked will stumble into ruin.

PROVERBS 24:16

Set

Arguments, fights and tantrums are a huge part of sports today. At every level, you can see these displays: Little league parents fight in the parking lot; players go into the stands; players and coaches ignore each other for days and weeks at a time. What causes all of this? Why can't we all just get along?

Most of the trouble lies within the selfish nature of humans. We have been trained to think that we are always right and that someone else is to blame. When an official makes a call against you, what do you do? Most of the time, you probably grumble, complain and point a finger at someone else.

"It's not my fault!" is the cry of the selfish warrior in battle. Excuses abound, but the truth is that you are not perfect. Yes, even *you* make a mistake now and then. In Proverbs 24:16, we read that even a righteous man falls seven times—and just lays there and wallows in his self-pity, right? No! "Though a righteous man falls seven times, *he will get up.*" Those who are righteous get up and admit that they were wrong.

Tough words are hard to say. The "W" word is not supposed to be a part of our vocabulary. Well, I hate to say it, but it needs to be there. Come on, say it with me: "I was wrong."

Admitting our mistakes in life will help us to develop into better people for God's service. So the next time you mess up, say this simple phrase and own up to your responsibility. And if necessary, add this to it: "I'm sorry."

Your actions and attitudes will make you either better or bitter. The choice is yours. No one likes to be wrong, but when you are, don't sit there in your sin and make excuses. Get up, own up, and live up! —*Jere Johnson*

Go

1. Why do you think it is so difficult for people to say the words "I was wrong"?
2. When was the last time that you admitted to someone else that you were wrong?
3. What can you do today to be accountable for your actions and attitudes?

Workout
Job 42:1-6; 1 John 1:8-10

Overtime
Lord, I don't want to be a bitter person, limited by my pride. Help me to admit when I have made a mistake or wronged another person. Help me to be like the righteous man who gets up after he falls. Thank You for Your abundant grace. Amen.

Lean on Me

Ready

Trust in the LORD forever, for the LORD,
the LORD, is the Rock eternal.

ISAIAH 26:4, *NIV*

Set

In 1992, the Olympic Games were held in Barcelona, Spain. Athletes from around the world gathered as they do every four years to compete against the best from every country. One such athlete was Derek Redmond. Representing England in the 400-meter, Redmond was considered a medal contender—until his semifinal heat.

The crowd in the packed stadium anticipated a great race from this champion runner. The race was moving along well with Redmond in the lead until . . . halfway down the backstretch, Redmond collapsed on the track with a pulled hamstring. As medical staff rushed toward him, Redmond struggled to get to his feet. He had only one thing on his mind—finishing the race.

In severe pain, Redmond made his way down the homestretch and was greeted by his father. With tears in his eyes, his father said, "Son, you do not have to do this." But the younger Redmond said that he had to finish the race. "Then lean on me," his loving father responded, "and we will finish this together." Staying in their lane to the end, the father and son finished the race.

Seeing his son's pain caused Redmond's father to do all he could to help his child. He knew that his son could not finish the race without him. God does the same for us. Through our prayers and petitions, when things get tough, God says, "I will help you finish! Lean on Me and I will see you through to the end."

There are many battles in life that you will not be able to handle on your own. Lean on the Father. Just as Redmond's father went to him in his time of need, so your heavenly Father will come to you when you call Him. When He comes to pull you through, swallow your pride and lean on Him. It is only through Christ that can we reach the finish line. —*Jere Johnson*

Go

1. Are you broken and alone?
2. Will you lean on Christ to help you through?
3. How can you lean on Christ today to lead you to victory in your life?

Workout

Psalm 30; Psalm 40; Matthew 5:3-4

Overtime

Father, thank You for always being there for me with Your arms wide open. You will always see me through to the end. I am never alone. Thank You for letting me lean on You all the time!

Obstacles and Opportunities

Ready

Send some men to explore the land of
Canaan, which I am giving to the Israelites.
From each ancestral tribe send one of its leaders.
So at the LORD'S command Moses sent them
out from the Desert of Paran.

NUMBERS 13:2-3, *NIV*

Set

When you walk onto a court to play a game, do you immediately think that you're going to lose or that you're going to win? Do you stare at your opponents while they warm up and begin to wonder why you even laced up your Nikes, or do you focus on giving your all? Do you see obstacles, or do you see opportunities?

In Numbers 13, the spies were sent into Canaan to check out the land. God had already given them great victories in battle and rescued them from tough situations. During the 40 days that they were evaluating the land, they could have seen a great opportunity, but they didn't.

Only two guys, Joshua and Caleb, thought that they could succeed in acquiring the land. The rest of the team did what I think many of us would have done: They saw a wall and a formidable opponent and said, "We don't think that we can do this!"

Well, that much is true. We can't, but God can. It's strange that the Israelites didn't remember the situations from which God had delivered them and the victories He had granted. They also forgot that God had commanded them to go into the land and that He had promised to give it to them. These were His words: "Send some men to explore the land of Canaan, which I am giving to the Israelites."

God has already given us much. We only need to receive what He has promised. We are so much like these Israelites when faced with challenging situations. But I pray that we can be more like Joshua and Caleb, who received and believed in the opportunity that God had given them. —*Fleceia Comeaux*

Go

1. When you compete, what obstacles do you see?
2. With God's help, how might these obstacles be turned into opportunities?
3. What practical steps can you take to increase your faith in God's plan for your life?

Workout
Numbers 13:26-30; Deuteronomy 31:8; 2 Corinthians 12:9

Overtime
Lord, help me to remember that through my doubt, I can see only obstacles, but through my faith in You, I can see opportunities. Allow me to increase this faith every day. Amen.

Ready

Let us be given vegetables to eat and water to drink.
Then examine our appearance and the appearance of
the young men who are eating the king's food, and deal
with your servants based on what you see.

DANIEL 1:12-13

Set

God created food for our bodies to give us energy, sustain life, prevent disease and facilitate healing. Our food choices will affect our mood, mental focus, physical performance, weight, immune system function, decision-making and appearance. Athletes today have access to more information with respect to eating for peak performance than ever before. In order to compete at our best, we must know exactly what to eat and when to eat it!

Daniel also wanted to know what to eat and when to eat it. He knew that the first portion of food served from King Nebuchadnezzar's table was offered to idols and that it would be unacceptable to partake of it. He was determined not to put anything into his body that would dishonor God. So he, along with Shadrach, Meshach and Abednego, stood by his convictions and ate nothing but vegetables and drank nothing but water! God blessed his decision.

In America today, over 65 percent of all adults are overweight. It would be easy to argue that they have been eating the "royal" food. In many cases, the royal food has become an idol of self-satisfaction and gluttony. As competitors for Christ, we are called to be good stewards of all that He has given us. The FCA Competitor's Creed states, "My body is the temple of Jesus Christ. I protect it from within and without. Nothing enters my body that does not honor the Living God."

Each one of us knows the basics of healthy eating. Isn't it time to truly commit to honoring God through what we eat? God will bless our decision and our performance on the field will certainly improve! —*Jimmy Page*

Go

1. How often do you eat foods that give you little nutrition?
2. Does your nutrition plan make you "healthier and better nourished" than other athletes?
3. What can you do to get your health back on track?

Workout

1 Corinthians 10:31

Overtime

Lord, I commit to honoring You through what I eat. Give me the wisdom to eat foods that lead to good health, high energy levels and peak performances. Amen.

Who, Me?

Ready

Whatever happens, conduct yourselves in a manner worthy of the gospel of Christ.

PHILIPPIANS 1:27, *NIV*

Set

Every team needs leaders on and off the field who set examples at practice, in the classroom and with their friends. Leaders show the way to work in all areas of their lives. However, many players do not want that responsibility.

When I share with athletes and encourage them to be leaders, I usually get the same response: "Who, me?" They feel that nobody is watching them and that no one cares what they do on or off the field. I beg to differ. Athletes are under the microscope. People are watching. Peers are watching. And fellow athletes are watching.

Paul knew this quite well. He understood that as believers in Christ, we are all called to lead. He challenges us in Philippians to live in a way that brings honor to Christ—not just to live our faith, but also to be an example to others.

Many believers feel that they are not spiritual leaders, but we all have that calling. No, we might not be called to lead a church or join the international missions, but we all have a mission field that surrounds us daily. We need to demonstrate Christlike leadership within our sphere of influence.

So, the next time you are tempted to respond, "Who, me?" to the opportunity to lead as an athlete or believer, remember that others are watching closely. Don't ruin your opportunity to show leadership by living a life that is unpleasing to God.

The best way to blow your witness is to talk one way and act another. Doing this affects every part of your life as an athlete and as a follower of Christ. Don't be the person that no one wants to follow because of your double standards.

Who, me? Yes, you! People want to follow the leadership of someone who will take them higher than they have ever been before. So let your actions be those that people will want to follow. Be a leader! Live the life of truth! —*Jere Johnson*

Go

1. Do you see yourself as a leader, or are you more likely to respond "Who, Me?" when someone asks you to lead?
2. Are you guilty of leading a double life as an athlete? As a believer?
3. How can you start to lead effectively for Christ today?

Workout
Matthew 5:13-16; James 2:14-26; 1 John 3:18-19

Overtime
Lord, I know I am able to lead, but I am scared. Please give me the strength to stand up for You each day. Help me to be not of this world, but of You only, Lord. Thank You for giving me Your grace to show others about You each day! Amen.

Conformity

Ready

Do not conform any longer to the pattern of this world,
but be transformed by the renewing of your mind.
Then you will be able to test and approve what God's
will is—his good, pleasing and perfect will.

ROMANS 12:2, *NIV*

Set

Abby was on cloud nine. As a freshman, she had just made the varsity girls' soccer team. She played hard during that freshman year, but when tryouts came at the beginning of her sophomore year, she assumed that she was guaranteed a spot on the team and put very little effort into what she was doing. As a result, Abby was cut from the team.

Abby's story has a clear parallel with our Christian walk. So many times we become complacent and feel that because we've accepted Christ, we've done our job. It's easy to just sit in FCA or in our youth groups, but what really matters is how we are pushing ourselves to become better Christians.

In Revelation 3:15-16 God tells us:

I know your deeds, that you are neither cold nor hot. I wish you were one or the other! So, because you are lukewarm—neither hot nor cold—I am about to spit you out of my mouth (*NIV*).

Halfway doesn't cut it with God. We have a world to save. We can't afford to be complacent! —*Heather Price*

Go

1. Have you ever been in a situation in which you just didn't care anymore about the outcome?
2. How can you learn to refocus on Christ during those times?

3. What do you need to do today to allow God to light a fire in your heart?

Proverbs 12:24; Matthew 25:1-13; Hebrews 6:9-12

Overtime
Lord, don't let me become complacent in my Christian walk. Place in my heart a fire that is unquenchable. I desire something more than a lukewarm relationship with You. Please renew my mind and my heart each day as I spend time with You and read Your Word. Amen.

$10 Million Tongue

Ready
With the tongue we praise our Lord and Father, and with it we curse men, who have been made in God's likeness. Out of the same mouth come praise and cursing. My brothers, this should not be.
JAMES 3:9-10, *NIV*

Set
As competitors, it is often hard to guard our mouths. Carson Palmer, a Heisman Trophy winner and the No. 1 NFL draft pick in 2003, signed a $49 million, 6-year contract with the Cincinnati Bengals. A total of $10 million of the deal was for his signing bonus.

However, that $10 million wasn't contingent upon his great throwing arm, his intelligence as a quarterback or his great play-calling. It was contingent upon his tongue and whether or not he would say anything negative about his team, coaches or management. Basically, the $10 million signing bonus was a loyalty pledge in which Carson guaranteed that he would not be critical. If he ripped into his team, he lost the cash. This was quite an incentive for him to keep his speech positive and encouraging.

In the heat of battle, it is difficult to keep our tongues from slipping. After someone has wronged us on the field or in the locker room, it is easy to lash out. God desires not only for us to keep our mouths from cursing but also to abstain from being critical.

There are two types of people in the world: builders and tearers. Builders use their words to lift up those around them. They make other people feel good about themselves. They pour into the emotional bank accounts of others. Tearers are people who berate those around them. They are the cut-down kings, usually saying things to make themselves look better in front of others.

The bottom line is that the tongue is only a reflection of what is in the heart. When the pressure comes, we speak what is in our heart. When you are under pressure, what comes out? Criticism or godliness? You might not get paid $10 million for having a Christlike tongue, but your Savior will be glorified! —*Dan Britton*

Go

1. What kind of person are you—a builder or a tearer? Which one would your friends and teammates say you are?
2. What came out of your heart the last time you were under pressure? How will you respond differently next time?
3. What does it mean to have a Christlike tongue? What are some specific ways that you could change what comes out of your mouth?

Workout

Proverbs 12:18; Proverbs 15:4; Ephesians 4:29; 1 Peter 3:10

Overtime

Lord, help me to be a person whose words build up those around me—those in my family, in my school, on my team and in my neighborhood. Create in me a clean heart, God. I desire to glorify You in all I say. Amen.

Ready

Finally, be strengthened by the Lord and by His vast strength. Put on the full armor of God so that you can stand against the tactics of the Devil.

EPHESIANS 6:10-11

Set

Under Armour sports performance apparel has become one of the hottest brands in sports. The company has "engineered" apparel for athletes to protect them from the cold, the heat and the turf. They even offer performance underwear! Athletes from the NFL to NASCAR—and even members of the military—wear Under Armour gear in order to protect themselves from the elements and to enhance performance. I have to admit that I rarely train without it! And my boys even wear it under their football, baseball and lacrosse equipment.

The website for the company confidently boasts, "The Under Armour brand on the chest is more than a logo, it's our guarantee . . . This shirt is doing something for you. This shirt is making you better."[2] According to the company, somehow this "armor" will actually make you perform better!

As competitors for Christ, we are given a different kind of armor. The FCA Competitor's Creed states, "My body is the temple of Jesus Christ. I protect it from within and without." Just as we protect our bodies through intense physical training, we must also protect our hearts and minds by putting on our spiritual armor. If we step onto the playing field without being prepared physically, our opponent is likely to dominate the competition. We are at a greater risk for injury, and we become a liability to our team. If we step onto life's playing field without the full armor of God, then our opponent, the devil, is likely to push us all over the field. We are at a greater risk for moral failure, and we become a liability to our team, Team Jesus Christ.

—Jimmy Page

Go

1. Would you ever compete without the right equipment?
2. How can failure to put on the armor of God make you a liability to Team Jesus Christ?
3. Do you put on your spiritual armor each day?

Workout

1 Thessalonians 5:8; Romans 13:11-14; Ephesians 6:10-17

Overtime

Lord, just as I put on my armor for competition, help me put on Your spiritual armor so that I can stand against the schemes of the devil and be protected from within. Amen.

Following Your Dreams

Ready

"For I know the plans I have for you," declares the LORD, "plans to prosper you and not to harm you, plans to give you hope and a future. Then you will call upon me and come and pray to me, and I will listen to you."

JEREMIAH 29:11-12, *NIV*

Set

As I stood in the phone booth, tears came to my eyes. I had just called my parents to let them know that I would be flying home that night to Los Angeles. The Cleveland Cavaliers had become the third straight NBA team that I had failed to make.

How could this happen? I had such high hopes of realizing my dream to play in the NBA when I was drafted out of the University of Iowa, but it was becoming clear to me that dreams don't always come true.

As the tears ran down my face, I thought that my days as a basketball player were over. I had lost my identity. Basketball was my life. What would the future hold now? I should have known that my future was in the hands of Someone bigger than myself. Yes, God was still in control, even if I was not aware of it.

It was shortly thereafter that I received an invitation to play full-time with a sports ministry team. For the next nine years I was able to travel the country (and the world) playing basketball and sharing my faith with thousands of people. The tears were long forgotten as God began using me in ways that I had never imagined.

Today, as I minister to leaders in our nation's capital, I am reminded daily that God still holds my future as well as the futures of those around me. I now know to hold plans loosely, resting securely in the knowledge that my Father may have a far different plan from my own. —*Dan Frost*

Go

1. What types of plans and dreams have you established for your future?
2. Are you willing to follow those plans and dreams no matter what the cost?
3. Are you willing to give up your plans and dreams if God's plans and dreams for you are different?

Workout
Proverbs 16:9; Matthew 6:33-34; Mark 8:34-36; Ephesians 2:10

Overtime
*Lord, thank You for setting the path before me, even if
I don't realize that it is the best road for me to take.
Help me to understand Your will and to surrender
my plans to You. Amen.*

Far More Important

Ready

You shall love the Lord your God with all your heart, with all your soul, with all your mind, and with all your strength . . . You shall love your neighbor as yourself. There is no other commandment greater than these.

MARK 12:30-31

Set

As a young athlete, I thought winning was everything. I wanted to win every time I competed. Whether it was a big high school game against our rivals or just a pick-up basketball game against my brothers, I wanted to win. The competitive juices would always flow through me. One of the greatest NFL coaches of all time, Vincent Lombardi, once said, "Winning isn't everything—but wanting to win is."[3] As an athlete, I had a lot of wanting, even though I didn't win every time.

In Mark 12:33, a religious teacher summarized Jesus' words by saying, "To love Him with all the heart, with all the understanding, and with all the strength, and to love one's neighbor as oneself, is far more important than all the burnt offerings and sacrifices." At that time, burnt offerings and sacrifices were important. But this man realized that there was nothing more important than loving God.

What could possibly be more important than loving God? Maybe for you it's not burnt offerings, but it could be your sport, your friends, your family, school work, the future or maybe even winning. Usually, there is something in our lives that tries to crowd out Jesus. Examine your heart today and ask God to show you what is keeping you from loving Him above all else. —*Dan Britton*

Go

1. Is there anything or anyone in your life more important than Jesus?
2. Would your best friend agree with your answer to the above question? What would Jesus say?

3. Vince Lombardi has his own perception of winning. What would be your personal definition of winning?

Workout
Deuteronomy 6:4-9

Overtime
Lord, I want nothing in my life to be more important than You. So many things try to crowd You out. Pour out Your wisdom and help me to see what those things are. You are first in my life. You are far more important than anything.

Leaving a Mark

Ready
I have been crucified with Christ and I no longer live, but Christ lives in me. The life I live in the body, I live by faith in the Son of God, who loved me and gave himself for me.
GALATIANS 2:20, *NIV*

Set
As an eight-year-old, I had a once-in-a-lifetime opportunity to ride my older brother's motorcycle. I wanted to show him how "big" I was, so I took off recklessly. About 100 yards down the dirt road, my front tire hit a hole. As I flew through the air, my life passed before my eyes. I landed in a ditch and the motorcycle landed on my back. Ouch!

Thankfully, as a result of my being in the ditch, the only part of the motorcycle that touched my back was the muffler. As the muffler burned through my shirt and my flesh, I experienced a world of hurt. I had been branded! Eventually, my brother rescued me, and I was banned from riding his bike again. Even though that event happened 28 years ago, I still have a nice burn mark on my back—an imprint made by that hot muffler.

An imprint is a permanent mark. It is an engraving, etching, impression or inscription. Every time I compete or coach, I leave an imprint. It can be either a good impression or a bad one, but that is up to me. The ultimate question is not whether I have left a good or a bad imprint, but whether I have left an imprint of myself or of Jesus. It is so true that the athlete or coach who is walking with Jesus will never leave an imprint of himself or herself, but only the imprint of Jesus. What a challenge!

Paul writes in Galatians 2:20 that we need to die to ourselves so that there will be no mark of us. When you are playing or coaching, be committed to leave behind the imprint of Christ! —*Dan Britton*

Go

1. When you compete, what kind of imprint do you leave?
2. Would those around you say that it is your imprint or Jesus' imprint?
3. What are some practical things that you can do to make sure the imprint will be the Lord's and not yours?

Workout
Ephesians 4:1; Colossians 1:10

Overtime
*Lord, I know that my goal is to compete in such a way
as to leave behind Your mark and not mine. It is hard, Lord.
I am always consumed with my own performance. Lord,
break me of the hold that competition has on me. My prayer is
that all who see me compete will know that it is all about You.
Transform me into Your agent of change.*

Ready

Let us fix our eyes on Jesus, the author and perfecter of our faith, who for the joy set before him endured the cross, scorning its shame, and sat down at the right hand of the throne of God.

HEBREWS 12:2, *NIV*

Set

Carolina Panthers quarterback Jake Delhomme didn't rush into the locker rooms after losing Super Bowl XXXVIII to the New England Patriots. Quite the contrary: He stood on the sidelines and forced himself to watch the Patriots in jubilee. "I guess I just wanted it to hurt as much as possible," Delhomme commented afterward. "I wanted to watch the celebration so that it could hurt, so I could remember it, for motivation."[4]

We've all experienced defeat in sports. Sooner or later, all of us will experience defeat in life through hurtful relationships, loss, confusion, bad choices, mistakes, regrets, lost opportunities and rejection. How do we endure such times in life? How do we keep the faith? These are the real questions to ask in such times.

The writer of Hebrews gives us at least one helpful answer: We should focus our eyes on Jesus. He suffered a painful, suffocating death on the cross—the symbol of utter shame in His day. Sometimes, focusing on the cross can be hard, especially when we get a glimpse of its reality. But the cross of Christ *is* hard—and it looks so much like defeat! The point is that remembering Christ's agony on the cross can sometimes push us forward. When we identify ourselves with Him in His death, we'll also identify with His resurrection. The cross and Christ's death actually become the hope of the world through His resurrection.

During life's beatings, try not to retreat to the locker room. Like Delhomme, stand on the sidelines and look to our Savior, who's been in our shoes and persevered through even the greatest lashings. The sight of Him will allow us to endure and carry us into tomorrow.
—*Kyle Shultz*

Go

1. What pain in your life are you turning your eyes from today?
2. How might facing the hurt help you?
3. What can you learn from Jesus when it comes to dealing with pain in your life?

Workout

Romans 8:18-21; Hebrews 12:3

Overtime

God, when I reflect on the sacrifice You made, the trials in my life pale in comparison. Just as You overcame death, I want to overcome the trials in my life with that same power. Amen.

Sweat Equity

Ready

You intended to harm me, but God intended
it for good to accomplish what is now
being done, the saving of many lives.

GENESIS 50:20

Set

A mutual respect exists among athletes. To some degree, as athletes we all have a single-minded, committed lifestyle that is laced with adversity. This is the price we pay to excel. An athlete's identity and purpose hinges on his or her performance, but what happens when adversity strikes?

What we see as adversity, God sees as opportunity. In Genesis 38–39, we read the story of how Joseph was sold into slavery by his own family and then imprisoned for 13 years for a crime he did not commit. But Joseph stood firm. "What men meant for evil, God used for good," he said (see Genesis 50:20). Joseph was right: Years after being sold into slavery, he became second in command over all of Egypt!

Adversity not only builds character, but also reveals it. In 1 Samuel 17, David, who was deemed too young to go to battle with his eight older brothers, cultivated his skills by fighting lions and bears while tending his flock. Armed with only a sling and stones, this small shepherd boy faced the giant that no other Israelite soldier dared to fight.

"You come against me with a dagger, spear, and sword," David said to the giant, "but I come against you in the name of the Lord of Hosts, the God of Israel's armies—you have defied Him. Today, the Lord will hand you over to me" (1 Samuel 16:45-46). David declared that the battle was the Lord's, and he defeated the mighty Goliath.

Playing ball meant the world to me as a young man. God had blessed me with natural ability and I excelled at every level. Then adversity struck. I was cut by the first NFL team that signed me. Down and out, I begrudgingly headed to Tampa Bay to play for the Bandits of the USFL. It was there that I met Jesus through the Bandits' chapel program. God then called me to youth ministry.

I am living proof that God can do great things with what we consider discouraging situations. Whether we have been deceived, beaten, jailed, surrounded by lions or cut from a team, we are being prepped through adversities for divine opportunity! —*Harry Flaherty*

Go

1. What adversities and challenges are you currently facing in your life?
2. What is being revealed about your character in the midst of these adversities?
3. How will you choose to view the current adversities that you are facing?

Workout
Genesis 50:15-21; 1 Samuel 17:45-47; Psalm 23

Overtime
Father, help me today to draw upon Your strength when facing adversity. Use these situations for Your glory and Your purpose.

Ready

We regard no one from a worldly point of view.
Though we once regarded Christ in this way, we do so
no longer. Therefore, if anyone is in Christ, he is a new
creation; the old has gone, the new has come!

2 CORINTHIANS 5:17, *NIV*

Set

There is a great Peanuts comic strip that shows Lucy about to catch a
fly ball. At the last minute, she loses sight of the ball and misses it. Lucy
turns to Charlie Brown and says that she is sorry, but the "past" got in
her eyes.

It is easy to let past mistakes get in the way of a good performance.
We remember what we have done wrong at the worst time in our lives
and end up making the same mistakes again. Then we begin the cycle
of rehearsing that mishap over and over in our mind.

As a Christian, instead of letting the past get in your eyes, turn your
eyes to the present and to the possibility of doing things the right way.
Remember, you are a new creation in Christ and you don't have to keep
making the same mistakes.

Being a new creation in Christ means that you are guaranteed forgiveness for all the mistakes that you have made in the past or that you
will make in the future. First John 1:9 describes how God responds
when we ask for His forgiveness: "He is faithful and just and will forgive
us our sins and purify us from all unrighteousness" (*NIV*). That is a
great promise and a great reason to stop rehearsing our past mistakes.

Instead of focusing on the past, turn your eyes to God—the audience of One—and to the present possibility of doing things right. Take
time to think about experiencing success and enjoying God's promises.
—*Dr. Julie Bell*

Go

1. What past mistakes do you continue to rehearse?
2. What prevents you from asking God for forgiveness?

3. Once you have asked for forgiveness, will you commit to accept God's forgiveness?

Workout
Psalm 103:12; Romans 8:1; Philippians 3:13-14

Overtime

Lord, I ask for Your forgiveness for any sin in my life.
Help me to focus on the "new" to come. Show me how
I can eliminate anything in my life that is getting in the way
of my relationship with You. Amen.

Failing?

Ready

Dear friends, let us love one another, for love comes from God. Everyone who loves has been born of God and knows God. Whoever does not love does not know God, because God is love.

1 JOHN 4:8, *NIV*

Set

It doesn't matter how good or how bad you are at sports. God is love. It doesn't matter whether you have all *A*s or all *F*s on your report card. God is love. But what exactly is love?

Love is patient, love is kind. It does not envy, it does not boast, it is not proud. It is not rude, it is not self-seeking, it is not easily angered, it keeps no record of wrongs. Love does not delight in evil but rejoices with the truth. It always protects, always trusts, always hopes, always perseveres. Love never fails (1 Corinthians 13:4-8, *NIV*).

Since God is referred to in the Bible as the very essence of love, this means that God Himself is patient and kind. God does not envy. He is not puffed up with pride. He does not behave rudely, does not seek His own, is not provoked, and does not rejoice in evil.

God rejoices in the truth. He bears all things, believes all things, hopes all things and endures all things. God never fails! Even when *you* fail, God never fails to love you, His child. So as you go through your day, think about how much God loves you.

For God so loved the world that he gave his one and only Son, that whoever believes in him shall not perish but have eternal life (John 3:16, *NIV*).

Live your life in love. After all, "we love because He first loved us" (1 John 4:19). —*Alex Harb*

Go

1. What are some of the ways that God has shown His incredible love in your life?
2. Who else in your life besides God loves you? Your family? Your friends?
3. How have you shown love to others? How can you improve on showing love to others?

Workout

Romans 5:8; 8:38-39; Ephesians 5:1-2; 1 John 4:7-21

Overtime

God, thank You for Your perfect, nonjudgmental love.
Help me to be a walking example of this love and show me
practical ways that I can love my friends and family.
I pray this in Jesus' name, Amen.

What God Hates

Six things the Lord hates; in fact, seven are detestable to Him: arrogant eyes, a lying tongue, hands that shed innocent blood, a heart that plots wicked schemes, feet eager to run to evil, a lying witness who gives false testimony, and one who stirs up trouble among brothers.

PROVERBS 6:16-19

Set

What enters your mind as you read the verses above, knowing that God hates the behaviors listed there? Do you find yourself thinking of times, perhaps even recently, when you have done something that God abhors? It's interesting (and convicting) that the Lord puts shedding innocent blood and spreading strife among brothers in the same list. To the world, shedding innocent blood is certainly considered much worse than creating conflict. But just what does it mean to stir up "trouble among brothers"?

"Strife" can be defined as "a bitter, sometimes violent conflict or dissension; an act of contention; exertion or contention for superiority."[5] On a sports team, this could take many forms. It could be a situation in which you turn one of your teammates against another player so that you'll end up on top. Even if the argument or hard feelings only exist between you and the other person, everyone on your team feels the tension, and that leads to strife.

Consider how you're treating your teammates and the other people in your life. If you're creating strife, ask the Lord for wisdom. Ask Him to help you behave differently and then act on the guidance He gives you. Also, talk to an adult whom you respect and who treats people with the respect and kindness you want to exhibit. —*Roxanne Robbins*

Go

1. Are you involved in any kind of strife on your team?
2. Are you the one creating this strife?

3. How can you mend the situation based on the principles that God teaches us in the Bible?

Workout
Matthew 5:21-24; 1 Thessalonians 4:1-11

Overtime
Father, as I read Proverbs 6:16-19, I am reminded that many of my actions are abhorred by You. I am guilty of manipulating my teammates and friends to get what I want. Please forgive me and show me the way to correct these actions. Cause them to be as detestable to me as they are to You. I pray all this in Your name, amen.

Wear the Colors

Ready
For I am not ashamed of the gospel, because it is God's power for salvation to everyone who believes, first to the Jew, and also to the Greek.
ROMANS 1:16

Set
I can still remember when my coaches handed out uniforms to those of us who had made the cut. We were all so proud to be wearing our school's colors. The best part was being able to wear our jerseys to school on game days. Being identified as part of the team somehow made each one of us walk a little taller.

And now I have the blessing of seeing my young sons experience that same thrill of putting on their uniforms and being part of a team. When they put on their jerseys, they seem to grow in confidence, as if they are truly part of something special.

My sons are proud to represent their teams. They know that their teammates are counting on them and that they can count on their teammates. They will give everything they've got. They will leave it all on the field!

The reality is that everyone likes to be identified with his or her favorite team. No matter what are your favorite teams, chances are good that you like to wear gear with their logo on it. We all like to "put on the uniform."

As competitors for Christ, we are called to put on His uniform. The FCA Competitor's Creed states:

> I am a Christian first and last.
> I am created in the likeness of God Almighty
> to bring Him glory.
> I am a member of Team Jesus Christ. I wear the
> colors of the cross.

If God passed out a jersey to everyone who was a part of His team, would you be proud to wear yours? Would you grow in confidence knowing that you were representing the Creator of the universe? Would it make you give everything you've got? Would you be proud to "wear the colors of the cross," or would you be ashamed? *—Jimmy Page*

Go

1. Are you as excited to be identified with Jesus as you are to be identified with your favorite sports team?
2. What are some practical ways that you can "wear the colors of the cross" when you are competing?
3. How will knowing that Jesus is on your team help you to be more confident when you compete?

Workout
Mark 8:38; 2 Timothy 1:7-8; 2:15

Overtime
Lord, help me to be eager to be identified with You. Help me to represent You in competition and in life, for I am not ashamed of the gospel!

Tunnel Vision

Ready

Brothers, I do not consider myself to have taken hold of it. But one thing I do: forgetting what is behind and reaching forward to what is ahead, I pursue as my goal the prize promised by God's heavenly call in Christ Jesus.

PHILIPPIANS 3:13-14

Set

"That's never been done here before."
"We've never been to the state playoffs."
"We've never beaten them before."

How many times have we as athletes looked at past seasons as the standard for potential success in the current season? The past can be a great thing when it is kept in the proper perspective. It can help teams play above their skill level simply because they are from a school with a good reputation. But it also can lead teams to sell themselves short.

At times we get caught up in looking at what has happened to us in the past. We seem to think that what we did last year has a bearing on what we can do this year. Yes, that is true to an extent. If you don't work hard in the off-season, the season's competition will be a struggle. But you also have to learn how to block past seasons out of your mind in order to reach your full potential.

Paul knew this all too well. He had been the ultimate bad guy. He not only persecuted Christians, but he also asked for letters that would allow him to kill them. How could someone with such a past be of any use in building up the kingdom of God? By "forgetting what is behind." Paul accepted God's grace and forgiveness and pressed on to the goal of what the Lord had for him. He refused to allow past mistakes to keep him from doing the will of the Father who had saved him from such a lifestyle.

If Paul, who had killed many Christians because of their faith, could accept God's forgiveness and put his past behind him, don't you think you can? —*Michael Hill*

Go

1. What from your past is keeping you from doing God's will for your life?
2. Have you accepted God's grace and forgiveness?
3. Do you need to talk to someone about how to let go of your past?

Workout

Jeremiah 29:11; Romans 3:23-24; 6:1-14; Hebrews 6:1

Overtime

Father, forgive me for my past mistakes and free me from the guilt that comes with them. Help me to focus on what is ahead instead of what is behind. Take this day that You have given me and use it for Your glory. Amen.

The Eternal Prize

Ready

Do you not know that in a race all the runners run, but only one gets the prize? Run in such a way as to get the prize. Everyone who competes in the games goes into strict training. They do it to get a crown that will not last; but we do it to get a crown that will last forever.

1 CORINTHIANS 9:24-25, *NIV*

Set

As a member of the sports media, I hear quite a few stories about athletes who build their entire lives around their sport. They eat, sleep, breathe and live specifically to achieve their personal athletic goals. It consumes so much of their mind that they don't focus on anything else.

But then something unexpected happens. It could be a variety of things: injury, illness, or whatever. Suddenly, they are stripped of the sport that had occupied so much of their time and energy. And when it's gone, they're left with nothing. Complete emptiness.

It is at this point that many athletes realize they need something more—something that can't be found in trophies or medals, something that is eternal. And this is exactly where God wants them.

God has brought them to that point for them to realize their need for Him and to show them that the things of this world are temporary. And that includes sports. Nothing will last forever except the crown of life that can only be found in a relationship with Jesus Christ.

What is your motivation for competing? Are your goals centered around record books, championships or trophies? Or are your sights set on a prize of more lasting value? Today, make sure that the most important race you are running is the one that offers the prize of eternity. Run to "get a crown that will last forever." —*Jill Ewert*

Go

1. Think back to a time when you achieved an athletic goal or were successful in a competition. How long did the joy of that achievement last?
2. How does the joy you experienced in that particular event compare to the joy of the Lord?
3. How would you react if your sport were taken away from you today?

Workout
Matthew 6:19-21; 2 Corinthians 5:14-15; Colossians 3:23-24

Overtime
God, help me to keep my eyes focused on the eternal prize. I want You to be first in my priorities and I want to compete for Your glory, not mine. In the name of Jesus, I pray. Amen.

Leave Your Mark

Ready

You yourselves are our letter, written on our hearts,
recognized and read by everyone, since it is plain that
you are Christ's letter, produced by us, not written with
ink but with the Spirit of the living God.

2 CORINTHIANS 3:2-3

Set

One of my favorite childhood memories came on my eleventh
birthday, March 15, 1972. I received a gift that set me head and
shoulders above everyone else in the neighborhood. It was something that made me the envy of all my friends. I received the
coolest bicycle in the world—a real "big boy" bike. I'm telling you,
it was so shiny and bright. It had a white frame with a blue glitter banana seat, blue glitter handles and tassels. It did indeed
make me the envy of all my friends. That bike made me the
coolest kid in the neighborhood. I might as well have been flying
an F-16 fighter jet. It was fast as lightning!

But the coolest thing about that bike was its blue tires. I was
the only kid in town who could lay blue streaks on the sidewalk.
The other kids could only lay black. We'd all line up together, race
down the sidewalk and then slam on our breaks to see who could
leave the longest mark. Mine was always blue. If there was a blue
streak on the sidewalk, you'd know I had been there. I had left my
mark, and everybody knew whose it was.

As Christians, God calls us to leave marks on the places that
we've been. We are called to influence others for Christ. Whether it
is at work, at home or around the neighborhood, God calls us to
live a life that reaches out to others and glorifies Him. We are
called to leave our marks on the people we come into contact with
each day, and that mark needs to look as much like Christ as possible. So today, ask yourself, What kind of mark are you leaving?
—Brad Holloway

Go

1. What opportunities do you have today to leave your mark?
2. What impact does it have on athletes and coaches when they see the mark that you have left behind?
3. Can you say that the mark you are leaving resembles Christ?

Workout

John 4:28; Acts 9:42; 1 Corinthians 2:1-5; Philippians 1:13

Overtime

Lord, help me to realize that the greatest goal I can reach is to make an eternal impact on the lives of those whom You have put in my path. Amen.

Setting an Example

Ready

We have put our hope in the living God,
who is the Savior of all men, and especially of those
who believe. Command and teach these things.
Don't let anyone look down on you because you are
young, but set an example for the believers in speech,
in life, in love, in faith and in purity.

1 TIMOTHY 4:10-12, *NIV*

Set

January 16, 2004, is a date that may have significantly impacted the sports world for many years to come. Two 14-year-old athletes made a big splash in their respective sports. Michelle Wie played in the Sony Open on the PGA tour and missed the cut by one stroke, tying two men who had won major championships the previous year. Freddy Adu, in a move that shocked no one, was chosen as the top pick in the Major League Soccer draft by D.C. United.

While Michelle Wie and Freddy Adu will be competing with and against athletes twice their age—and some old enough to be their parents—they can still make an impact by the example they set. I believe that this is what leading those who are above you is primarily about. For example, when Adu was given the number 9 on his jersey, he responded by saying, "I would rather have number 11, but you can't always get what you want. You have to earn it."[6]

It would have been easy for the 14-year-old phenom to whine and complain about not getting his number. Doing so, I believe, would have stripped any credibility and influence that Adu has with his coaches, teammates and fans. Instead, he set an example that reveals a desire to work hard and be a team player.

Whether you are young in age or young at heart, people are watching you to see how you live, not how you say you live. What kind of example are you going to set for them? —*Josh Carter*

Go

1. What kind of example are you setting for others on your team?
2. Of the five areas that Paul talks about (speech, life, love, faith and purity), which area of your life needs the most improvement?
3. What can you do specifically to improve in this area?

Workout
Psalms 103:5; 119:9; Ecclesiastes 12:1; 2 Timothy 2:22

Overtime
God, just as it reads in 1 Timothy 4:12, I want to be an example for the believers in speech, in life, in love, in faith and in purity. Please do a supernatural work in my life so that each day, as I spend time with You in the Word, I will get a little closer to this goal. In Your name I pray, amen.

Commitment 101

Ready

All a man's ways seem right in his own eyes,
but the Lord weighs the motives. Commit your activities
to the Lord and your plans will be achieved.

PROVERBS 16:3

Set

"Commitment" is a big buzz word in sports today. Coaches are asking for commitment, players want to be committed, and schools are looking for a four-year commitment. But commitment is a word that is used very loosely today. (I personally believe that we need more athletes who are committed to their academic success before their athletic careers, but I'm old school on that one.)

When it comes to commitment, Jesus Christ wants us to be committed as well. He desires our commitment. When is the last time you said, "Lord, I am committing this to You!"

In the verse above from Proverbs, we read that if we commit our work to the Lord, our plans will succeed. Now, that does not mean we will win, but that we will be successful. When we walk with the Lord, we are guaranteed ultimate victory with Him in the end.

Committing everything to the Lord is a moment-by-moment adventure, not just a "once and done." Everything we do, everything we are and everything about us needs to be completely committed to Christ. You might say that sounds like a lot to ask, but it is the *only* way that we can be totally committed to Christ. Anything less just doesn't add up.

Are you struggling with commitment in life? If so, first commit all that you are to Christ and then go from there. Once you are fully committed to Him, things will work out in the end. —*Jere Johnson*

Go

1. How committed are you?
2. In terms of percentage, how committed are you to Christ?

3. How can you start being committed to Christ with all that you are?

Workout
Psalm 37:4-6; 1 Peter 4:19; Revelation 3:15-16

Overtime
Lord, today I commit to You. Help me to integrate this commitment into every part of my life so that I will be successful. Please bring friends into my life who can help keep me accountable as I live out my commitment to You. Amen.

Teammates

Ready
Watch your life and doctrine closely.
Persevere in them, because if you do, you will
save both yourself and your hearers.
1 TIMOTHY 4:16, *NIV*

Set
Chad was the consummate team player. He worked harder than everyone else. He was humble and unselfish, and never once did I hear him talk trash to an opponent. I knew there was something different about Chad, but I couldn't quite figure out what it was.

At age 16, I began to search for the purpose of my existence. Sports were gratifying, but I knew they wouldn't last forever. Around this time, I learned that the difference between Chad and me was that he had a personal relationship with Jesus Christ. This influenced his life on and off the field.

Through the connection I had with Chad as a fellow competitor and teammate, his life had a huge influence on my decision to give my life (sports and all) to Jesus Christ. Without the bond we had through sports, Chad would not have influenced my life the way he did.

The celebration of victories, the disappointment of tough losses, the sweat and the sacrifices all helped us to develop a strong relationship and opened my heart to see and hear the message of Christ through Chad.

As a Christian competitor, I encourage you to view your team as your mission field. Jesus Christ is calling you to be His ambassador and to help reconcile your teammates to God. —*Josh Carter*

Go

1. How have your teammates influenced your life? In what ways are you influencing your teammates?
2. How would you describe the bond you share with your teammates?
3. Can you identify one teammate for whom you will pray and into whose life you will intentionally pour Christ's love through your words and actions?

Workout

2 Corinthians 5:16–6:2; Colossians 4:2-6; 1 Peter 3:15

Overtime

God, I want to influence my teammates the way Chad influenced his. Please help me live in such a way that my teammates notice that there is something different about me. Open up opportunities for me to share about Your love for each of us and the forgiveness that covers our sins. Please use me to make a difference in this world. Amen.

Awestruck

Ready

All of a sudden, when the whole crowd saw Him,
they were amazed and ran to greet Him.

MARK 9:15

Set

In 1996, I went to my first professional golf tournament. Lush green grass, beautiful colors and the world's best golfers took center stage at Southern Hills Country Club in Tulsa, Oklahoma. I watched several groups tee off and was amazed at how far they hit the ball.

As I walked the course, I came to a hole where there was quite a buzz. People were crowding in to see a young golfer hit the ball—a young man named Tiger Woods. I, too, greatly admired this young, talented golfer. Tiger took it all in stride. He showed amazing composure for such a young player.

As Jesus was nearing the end of His public ministry, He, too, often drew quite a crowd. When people saw His disciples, they started to come together, but when they saw the Master Teacher, they would run to get close to Him. Did He ever tire of the crowd and people everywhere? I am sure He did at times, but He rarely showed it.

People gathered because they knew that when Jesus was around, something big was about to happen. People grew to expect great things from Christ every time they saw Him. And He never disappointed them. He continually amazed them with His goodness, His grace and His Godness! Truly, they were awestruck!

Today people still flock to see Tiger Woods play. They expect greatness every time, every shot, every hole. But Tiger is not God. He may be able to pull an eagle out of his bag, but I've never seen him (or his golf ball) walk on water. Remember, Tiger is just a man, but Jesus is *the* Man—Son of Man and Son of God. He deserves our awe! We should be awestruck when we reflect on Him. When Jesus is near today, do you run to see Him? —*Jere Johnson*

1. What athlete or coach are you in awe of?
2. How would you have reacted if you saw Christ coming?
3. How can you become more awestruck by your Savior?

Workout
Deuteronomy 28:10; 1 Samuel 12:18; Psalm 2:11; Habakkuk 3:12

Overtime
*Lord, I know that You are the famous one. Your name is
the name above all other names. Today, allow me to be
awestruck as I reflect upon Your greatness. Let me remember
that no one compares to You.*

Should Have Listened

Ready
At the end of your life, you will lament when
your physical body has been consumed, and you
will say, "How I hated discipline, and how my heart
despised correction. I didn't obey my teachers or
listen closely to my mentors."

PROVERBS 5:11-13

Set
"It's ok. They won't hurt you."
"It will make you better, bigger, stronger."
"Don't worry, no one will ever know . . ."

These are some of the phrases that student-athletes hear when they
are encouraged to take steroids. The pursuit of greatness is so powerful today that many athletes—young athletes—are doing things that
put their lives in jeopardy. I am sure that there are two voices they are
hearing, but there is only one that they should be listening to.

Proverbs 5 addresses the topic of staying away from things that are bad for you. In verse 13, you hear the remorse of someone who wishes he had listened to the wise advice he received instead of choosing to follow the crowd and his own evil desires. This sad story rings true in sports and in society today. Today, athletes are getting wise counsel from coaches, trainers, parents and pastors, but they are also getting advice from those who do not have their best interests at heart.

Whether the struggle is with steroids, drugs, drinking, pornography or something else, athletes must choose to listen to wise advice. It is crucial! They often want to choose immediate gratification over long-term goals, but it is the *eternal*—not the *internal*—that really matters. Coaches who push athletes to take steroids so that they can win more games are beyond foolish. Athletes who push their teammates to do things that will ultimately hurt them are not true teammates.

Listen only to those individuals who truly want what is best for you athletically, socially, academically and, most important, spiritually. Don't be the one to say, "I should have listened." By then it will be too late! —*Jere Johnson*

Go

1. Are you having a hard time listening to the right voices?
2. In your pursuit of better results, have you been guilty of doing things the wrong way?
3. How can you start today to listen to the right voices in your life?

Workout
Proverbs 5; James 1:19

Overtime
Father, I want to make wise decisions. Tune my ear to recognize when I am receiving unwise counsel so that I can make the right choice. Place people in my life who can support me and counsel me with godly wisdom. Help me to keep my focus on eternal things. Thank You for the protection of Your Holy Spirit. Amen.

Ready

That is what the Son of Man has done: He came to serve, not be served—and then to give away his life in exchange for the many who are held hostage.

MATTHEW 20:28, *THE MESSAGE*

Set

I was watching an interview on ESPNews with Barry Bonds. The topic was steroids. Bonds's personal trainer was one of four men recently charged in a steroid-distribution ring that allegedly supplied dozens of professional athletes with banned substances.

Athletes at all levels these days are doing all they can to get the edge. Nutritional supplements—some legal and healthy, others not—are widely used to give athletes an extra boost, better workouts and faster strength gain.

But what are the supplements of our spiritual lives? What does the spiritual steroid (without the negative connotation) look like? How do we get a boost?

There are many answers that would work here. But as I thought about my own experience, one thing popped into my mind: serving. Some of the greatest boosts in my spiritual life have occurred when I served on mission trips.

Back in high school, my youth group would take a mission trip every summer. There was one purpose: to serve others. Whether we were helping to build a church or hosting backyard Bible clubs, the focus was to serve.

Many people thought that we would come back from our mission trips exhausted, but we always came back energized and impassioned to live out the good news. What seemed to be an emptying of ourselves in service to others actually ended up boosting our faith and strengthening our hearts. Those service trips were always like 'roids for the soul.

Jesus called His disciples by saying, "Follow Me." His life was one of complete love and service. So if you need a boost today, try serving someone. —*Kyle Shultz*

1. Have you devoted time to serving someone else?
2. How were you and that person blessed by that time?
3. How can you serve others today through Christ's love?

Workout

John 12:26; Galatians 5:13; Ephesians 6:7-8; 1 Peter 4:10

Overtime

Lord, give me a heart of service—a heart that is willing to serve on and off the court. Show me the needs and help me to fill them. I love You, Lord, and I thank You for giving me opportunities every day to glorify and honor You. Amen.

In His Eyes

Ready

My soul, praise the Lord, and all that is within me, praise His holy name. My soul, praise the Lord, and do not forget all His benefits. He forgives all your sin; He heals all your diseases. He redeems your life from the Pit; He crowns you with faithful love and compassion. He satisfies you with goodness; your youth is renewed like the eagle.

PSALM 103:1-5

Set

If you tried to count on your hands the number of times someone let you down or you let someone else down, you'd run out of fingers. As humans, we fail miserably all the time. Thankfully, there are promises in the Bible such as the one in Psalm 103:12: "As far as the east is from the west, so far has He removed our transgressions from us."

There is incredible power in looking at ourselves through the eyes of Christ. No matter the mistake, the loss, the pain or the regret, in God's eyes we shine brightly. When you feel inadequate, depressed or ashamed, feel His presence. He redeems your life, rescues you from the pit and showers you with love and compassion. He satisfies your desires with awesome and wonderful things.

No matter where you've been or what you've done, God can restore you. Take a peek at yourself through His eyes—the eyes of grace and love. —*Danny Burns*

Go

1. What causes you to be ashamed of the actions that you have done in your life?
2. Do you realize that you are loved by God and that He has forgiven you?
3. What can you do to become the bright creation that God sees?

Workout
Luke 15:1-7; Romans 5:1-11

Overtime
God, it's so hard to fathom the pain in Your eyes as You watch me do what You despise. Yet through it all, Lord, Your love endures forever. Your grace and mercy are unexplainable. Lord, change me. Draw me close to You, Jesus, and restore me.

"Who is a God like You,
removing iniquity and passing over rebellion
for the remnant of His inheritance?
He does not hold on to His anger forever,
because He delights in faithful love.

He will again have compassion on us;
He will vanquish our iniquities.
You will cast all our sins
into the depths of the sea"
(Micah 7:18-19).

Ready
Let us fix our eyes on Jesus.
HEBREWS 12:2, *NIV*

Set

I had set my blocks for the 110-meter hurdles and taken a couple of practice starts. The starter called out, "Runners to your marks!" In my pre-race nervousness, I turned to my left and right to compare myself to the other runners. It was then that I noticed that the line I was using for the start was a full meter behind all of the other runners. I then made the fateful decision to keep my feet in my blocks while moving both hands up even with the other runners. I was nearly lying flat when the gun went off. I crawled out of the blocks and hit almost every hurdle. I finished second to last!

Where did I go wrong? I took my eyes off the finish line and began to compare myself with the other runners. I was trying to compete the way that others were competing instead of running my own race.

In sports, it is easy to compare ourselves to others rather than play our individual games in the way that we have practiced. We try to make someone else's unique ways our ways. But focusing on another person's game prevents us from focusing on our game and competing the way that God created us to compete. This does not mean that we should have the mentality of a loner and neglect the team for our own personal benefit; rather, competing the way that God created us to compete means that we work to develop our own unique skills so that we can be the best that we have been created to be.

Spiritually speaking, when do we get off track? When we take our eyes off Jesus—the finish line—and begin comparing ourselves to others. Stop the comparisons and play your game. Compete the way that you have prepared to compete. Be committed to developing your skills and your unique abilities so that your game is at its best and you reach the finish line having run *your* race. —*Kerry O'Neill*

Go

1. In what areas are you comparing yourself to others rather than fixing your eyes on Christ?
2. Why do you think that you are making this comparison?
3. How does this negatively affect your spiritual life?

Workout

Psalm 18:29-30; Mark 8:34-35; Colossians 3:23-24

Overtime

Lord, thank You for making me a unique creation. Help me to delight in that uniqueness today and to use the abilities You have given me in the way that You see fit. Amen.

In Him

Ready

Some take pride in a chariot, and others in horses, but we take pride in the name of the Lord our God.

PSALM 20:7

Set

On the second Sunday of every March, you will hear teams all over the country proclaiming how they should be invited to the NCAA Basketball Tournament. More than 30 teams get automatic bids through conference tournament championships, but 34 other teams have to be invited. These teams boast of the great things they have done—and how they deserve to be in the tournament.

During the Old Testament times, things weren't much different. Nations would boast of their great armies or warriors and how powerful they had become—as if they had risen to power on their own. Countless passages in Scripture describe how vain these people were and how God brought them to their knees each time. God wants us to understand that all we are and all we can become are only because of His work in our lives. It is only in Him that we can boast.

Although teams and individual athletes have reason to be proud of what they have accomplished, we all must understand that our abilities come from heaven above. The FCA Competitor's Creed states:

I do not trust in myself.
I do not boast in my own abilities or believe in my own strength.
I rely solely on the power of God.

Again, it is through God that we receive the power to perform. When we stop looking for praise and start giving it to Him, we will fully understand His power and goodness in our lives.

Teams, coaches and athletes today can stop looking to self-promote and instead boast in what God has gifted them to do: use all they are for His glory! —*Jere Johnson*

Go

1. Is it all about you and what you can do as an athlete?
2. Do you truly know who should get the credit for your accomplishments?
3. How can you start to live and compete for God today?

Workout
Joshua 24:15; Acts 8:4-25; Romans 3:27-31

Overtime
Lord, as I compete today against the evils of this world, may I give You all of the credit for what You have created me to do in You. You are awesome, Lord. Thank You for giving me the ability to worship You with my sport. I desire to honor only You with my performance today and every day. Amen.

Salty

You are the salt of the earth. But if the salt loses its saltiness, how can it be made salty again? It is no longer good for anything, except to be thrown out and trampled by men.

MATTHEW 5:13, *NIV*

Set

If you run around the soccer field for 90 minutes, you tend to sweat a lot. When you sweat excessively, your body loses much of its natural salt. Without salt in your body, you cannot stay hydrated. Being "salty" is an important part of being able to compete at a high level.

In the same respect, without a relationship with Jesus, you cannot absorb and learn from His Word. Learning God's ways by reading the Bible will impact your approach to competition, but not until you give your life fully to God and accept what His Son did for you on the cross.

If you have never done this, take a moment to pray and thank God for sending Jesus to die on the cross for all that you have ever done wrong. Then ask God to take control of your life. Allowing Jesus to take control might be painful at first (just like putting salt water on an open wound), but the healing and transformation will be incredible—better than you could ever imagine!

Mark 9:50 says, "Salt is good, but if it loses its saltiness, how can you make it salty again? Have salt in yourselves, and be at peace with each other" (*NIV*). Mark is comparing the importance of having salt in our bodies with the importance of having God in our lives.

When you give your life to Jesus and let the Holy Spirit work in your life, you will begin to understand God's teachings. You will begin to learn what it means to give God glory in all that you do and to be an example of His love to others. Let the Holy Spirit work inside of you so that those on your team and those watching can see God's love through you.

So how is your "salt" level? —*Amanda Cromwell*

Go

1. What are your thoughts about giving your life to God?
2. How does God impact your approach to your sport?
3. How might having more salt in your spiritual diet affect the way you compete?

Workout

Luke 14:34; John 4:4-14; 6:35; 15:5

Overtime

Father, thank You for sending Your Son to die for my sins. I surrender my life to You.

Team Player

Ready

Then he called the crowd to him along with his disciples and said: "If anyone would come after me, he must deny himself and take up his cross and follow me. For whoever wants to save his life will lose it, but whoever loses his life for me and for the gospel will save it.

MARK 8:34-35, *NIV*

Set

We were having an intersquad scrimmage and I was standing among a group of athletes, waiting to find out which team I would be on. I was sure that I would be placed on the team with the best athletes in the school, who were also my best friends. But instead, I was chosen to join a team that was considered to be the underdogs. In my anger and disgust, I told the coach that I was going to quit and began walking off of the field.

To my surprise, the coach let me go. I had been so sure that he would try to stop me, but he didn't. As I continued walking away slowly, I started thinking, *What am I going to tell my parents? And what are my friends going to think of me?*

Suddenly, I came to my senses, went back and joined the team. Guess what? Our team won the scrimmage, and I apologized to the coach for not trusting that he knew what he was doing.

We must always remember to look at the big picture. It's not about us, and it's not about what we want. Being on God's team means denying what we want and following Him. He strategically places us in situations in life in which we can make the greatest impact, even if this sometimes means being separated from things that we want and the people who are most familiar to us.

Remember, you have been created to make a difference, and your team's ability to win may just possibly lie within you. —*Carl Miller*

Go

1. What traits do you bring to your team that will make a difference?
2. Can you think of a time that you thought would be the worst experience of your life but turned out to be one of the best?
3. How willing are you to give up your rights and desires for the sake of your team?

Workout

Mark 10:29-30; John 15:16; 1 Corinthians 1:27-29

Overtime

God, help me to deny my own selfish desires, even when I am placed in situations that are not comfortable for me. I want to bring You honor in all that I do. Help me to look past what I want so that I can use the talent that You have given me to make a difference for the team on which I have been placed. Amen.

Ready

You show that you are a letter from Christ,
the result of our ministry, written not with ink but
with the Spirit of the living God, not on tablets
of stone but on tablets of human hearts.

2 CORINTHIANS 3:3, *NIV*

Set

As I approached the third hurdle, I knew that I was a little too far away to take it with my right leg. So in a split second, I decided to alternate and go over with my left foot leading. I had done this a thousand times in my career, but this time when I landed I felt my knee shift out of the socket. I had hyperextended my knee, and I knew my running days were over.

Surrounded by my teammates, I was faced with a choice. My team knew me as the person who had led them in Bible studies and professed Christ, and now they waited expectantly to see what was going to proceed out of my mouth. In a split second their anxious eyes received the answer when I screamed, "Hallelujah!" I yelled it from the sheer pain I was feeling.

The apostle Paul writes that as believers, we must be a living testimony—an open book for the world to see the glorious gospel of Jesus Christ. Sometimes this is painful. Sure, it could be physically painful, like the pain that I was feeling. Harder still, it could be psychologically painful, like the pain we feel when we are isolated from our peers because of our beliefs in Christ Jesus. Paul further writes that while he has gained much in the world, he counts it loss to him, so he might win Christ (see Philippians 3:8).

Although I would later need to have my left leg amputated from the accident, there was a greater outcome than I could have anticipated: Two people gave their lives to Christ as a result of seeing the way that I reacted to the situation. As Paul said, it was not I but Christ who lives inside who won the victory that day (see Galatians 2:20). —*John Register*

Go

1. Are you a living testimony for the world to see the glorious gospel of Christ? Why or why not?
2. How can you become more available to model Christ in your pain today, inside and outside of competition?
3. Are you able to say that having Christ in your life is worth the loss of everything else?

Workout

2 Chronicles 12:9-10; John 15:2; Philippians 3:8; Hebrews 10:35

Overtime

Father, help me to grow in You so that my life—each action that I perform and word that I speak—will bring You glory and honor. Amen.

Personal Best

Ready

God has put the body together, giving greater honor to the less honorable, so that there would be no division in the body, but that the members would have the same concern for each other. So if one member suffers, all the members suffer with it; if one member is honored, all the members rejoice with it. Now you are the body of Christ, and individual members of it.

1 CORINTHIANS 12:24-27

Set

What position is the most important in the game of football? What about in volleyball? And in baseball? There is a common misconception in team sports that the most important position on a team is the one that is played by the person who gets the most headlines or touches the ball the most. However, these are not always the most important roles on a team.

So what is the most important? The answer is simple: It's the one that you have been asked to play. God's Word states that whatever you are asked to do, you should do it with all your might (see Ecclesiastes 9:10).

If you are playing offensive guard and you don't block your assignment, the whole team pays the price. If you are a second-stringer and you don't put forth your best effort in practice, the whole team suffers. In volleyball, the hitters will never even touch the ball without a good pass from the back row.

Paul tells us in 1 Corinthians 12 that a body cannot function as it was designed to without its many parts working together. We should not consider one part of the body to be more important than another, nor should we believe that the role we have been asked to play is insignificant.

In both sports and life, the most important role is the one that you are asked to play. It is significant. Give your best each and every play. The team is depending on you! —*Joe Outlaw*

Go

1. What is your role on your team or in your line of work? What is your role in life?
2. Have you ever felt that your role wasn't important? Have you considered why your role would even exist if it wasn't important?
3. According to Scripture, how should your attitude change regarding your role in life?

Workout
1 Corinthians 12:12-27; Colossians 3:17,23-24

Overtime
Lord, thank You that I am on Team Jesus Christ. You have blessed me with gifts and talents, and I want to use them on Your team. I am grateful that I am one of a kind and that nobody else can play the role I can. Thank You, Jesus, for blessing me and giving me the privilege to serve.

Ready

But just as he who called you is holy,
so be holy in all you do.

1 PETER 1:15, *NIV*

Set

In the height of his playing days, Charles Barkley *claimed* that he was not a role model.[7] The University of Colorado *claimed* that the troubles with its football program were not as bad as they seemed.[8] Coach Nueheisel *claimed* that his gambling was no big deal.[9] The people involved in these situations did not want to be held to a higher standard. Why? Because they felt that athletics and off-the-field issues should be kept separate.

In many ways, that may be true. However, as athletes, we need to remember that we are who we are. People don't view Alex Rodriguez as just another guy who lives in New York; they see him as a future Hall of Famer who plays third base for the Yankees. As an athlete at any level, we are held to a higher standard. How we react to the spotlight demonstrates to others who we truly are.

Likewise, as believers in Christ, we are held to a higher standard, and we should strive to live up to that standard every day. Too many Christians compare themselves to others and just get by in their faith. But that is not God's standard for us. Our plan may be to slide by, but His plan for us is perfection. In 1 Peter 1:15, we learn that we need to be holy in all we do, just as God is holy. Our goal should be to be like Him. He set the standard, and we are called to follow it.

Some athletes and coaches today are setting standards of great worth and measure. Others are setting standards that are only worthy of the tabloids. But there is only one true standard by which we all will be measured one day—God's higher standard! So set your sights upward, plant your feet on the straight and narrow path, and make your actions worthy of Christ. If you strive for this standard, everything you do will be worth it all. —*Jere Johnson*

Go

1. Are you living your life below God's standard?
2. What is stopping you from striving for a higher standard?
3. How can you start to live by God's higher standard today?

Workout

Romans 12:2; 1 Corinthians 3:18-19

Overtime

God, I want to live by a higher standard, and I know that I will only be able to do this by allowing You to have complete control in my life. Guide me in Your ways. Amen.

Trust

Ready

Take delight in the Lord, and He will give you your heart's desires. Commit your way to the Lord; trust in Him, and He will act, making your righteousness shine like the dawn, your justice like the noonday.

PSALM 37:4-6

Set

Upon arriving in Atlanta for the National Wheelchair Championships, the stewardess informed me that they had forgotten my manual wheelchair in Minneapolis when I had changed planes. Fortunately, they had remembered to load my racing chair, but it arrived with a huge crack in the back wheel frame. I knew that there was no way I'd be racing with that!

As I sat in the claims office, filing reports on these two wheelchairs, I thought back to some verses that I had memorized from Psalm 56:3-4:

When I am afraid,
I will trust in You.
In God, whose word I praise,
in God I trust; I will not fear.
What can man do to me?

These verses calmed my heart. I didn't know if I'd be racing, but I knew that God was in control of everything.

The next day, my daily wheelchair arrived at camp. As it happened, my racing wheelchair manufacturer was also at the meet and had, on hand, an exact replacement for my broken wheel.

I was able to compete at that event and ended up setting national records in four events. That was neat. But the most exciting part of this experience was confirming that I could trust God, even when circumstances seemed out of control. *—Judy Siegle*

Go

1. Can you think of a situation in which things seemed out of control for you or your team?
2. On a scale of 1 to 10, how would you rank your trust level in this situation?
3. Can you list some of the occasions when God has provided for you during challenging times?

Workout

Joshua 1:9; Romans 9:33; Philippians 4:6-7

Overtime

God, many times I allow my frustration to control my attitude and actions. Help me to remain flexible when things aren't going my way. Help me to trust You more. Amen.

Ready

If you stop listening to instruction, my son, you will stray from the words of knowledge.

PROVERBS 19:27

Set

A wise man once said, "When you are through learning, you are through!" I don't know who actually said that, but my father used to repeat it to me often. As he would patiently try to teach his sons how to play different sports, he would catch us occasionally not paying attention. We would make simple mistakes that, if we had been listening, wouldn't have been made.

Solomon was a wise man—the wisest in all the land, some contended. He could've easily thought that he had arrived and had gained all the knowledge he needed, but he understood this simple concept: If you don't pay attention, listen and learn, you won't get the knowledge you need to further your understanding in life. We can learn a lesson from Solomon and other believers of his day. Learning was not just for young people; it was a lifetime process.

Great men in sports and history, such as John Wooden, Tony Dungy and my father, Jim Johnson, understand that listening and learning are daily tasks. You should never stop learning. So what are some practical things you can do to continue getting valuable instruction and knowledge?

First, get into God's Word every day. There is no better book to study in order to gain knowledge. Second, surround yourself with men and women who have "been there" and "done that" in the right ways. They are a wealth of wisdom and knowledge. Third, pray and ask the Lord to point you in the right direction!

Remember the line from my father at the beginning of this devotion? Well, it has come full circle, and my kids are now hearing the same message from me. And my prayer is that neither they nor I nor *you* ever stop listening and learning. —*Jere Johnson*

Go

1. Are you done learning and listening? Do you act like you are?
2. In what area in your life could you learn more?
3. Today how can you start learning more from God's Word?

Workout

Proverbs 1:5; 12:15; 19:20; James 1:19-25

Overtime

Lord, I don't ever want to stop learning. Show me where I need to be more teachable in my life, and surround me with men and women who will speak truth to me. And as I spend time reading the Bible, open my heart to Your instruction. Amen.

Looking Ahead

Ready

Not that I have already reached the goal or am already fully mature, but I make every effort to take hold of it because I also have been taken hold of by Christ Jesus.

PHILIPPIANS 3:12

Set

After routing Oklahoma University for its second straight national title, USC coach Pete Carroll was asked when preparation for the next season would begin. Carroll replied:

> "It's already going. We live this thing. If you're competing, then you're always competing. That's just part of it . . . I have people tell me, 'Just relax.' Don't tell me to relax. I'm having a . . . ball. We get to do this for six months, be on top of the college football world. We'll likely have a great chance at being the No. 1 team coming into next year. Shoot, that's awesome, awesome stuff."[10]

Carroll had just led his team to an undefeated championship season, yet he already had his sights set on the highest goals for the following year.

People in sports know what it means to have goals. Athletes set goals all the time with the belief that good goals will help them live up to their potential. At this time of the year, many are doing the same thing with life in general.

Some look ahead, merely wondering what the year will bring. Some look ahead without passion or vision at all. Still others look ahead in much the same way as Pete Carroll—they have a dream and want to be active in accomplishing it.

What would you like to see happen over the next year? Regardless of what this is, I encourage you to do two things: First, give it serious thought. What do you truly want to see happen? This can involve more than one answer. Second, write these things down.

Those of us who want everything that God has for us should stay focused on that goal. If you have something else in mind, something less than total commitment, God will clear your blurred vision—you'll see it yet! —*Kyle Shultz*

Go

1. What goals do you want to see happen next year?
2. Have you written these goals down and prayed about them?
3. What is God telling you to set as a goal for your life?

Workout
2 Corinthians 5:17; Philippians 3:12-21

Overtime
Lord, I realize that vision is a picture of the future that produces passion within my heart. It is sometimes hard to think about tomorrow, much less next year. Reveal to me what You want from me as a follower—what Your goals are for me, not what my goals are for You. I see the future with human eyes, but You desire me to see with spiritual eyes. Stretch my vision and show me not what is, but what can be.

No Pain, No Gain

Ready

I do not run like one who runs aimlessly,
or box like one who beats the air. Instead,
I discipline my body and bring it under
strict control, so that after preaching to others,
I myself will not be disqualified.

1 CORINTHIANS 9:26-27

Set

All athletes need to go through this, but most would probably rather skip it if it were possible. It's probably the part of sports that is the least fun. Yet this is also the part that separates average athletes from top athletes.

Have you figured it out yet? It's training. Athletic training involves many different things. Proper eating, weight training and practicing are all necessary in order to get into top playing condition.

As Christians, we need to be training ourselves spiritually. This involves getting sin out of our lives and removing those things that may not be sin but are a hindrance in our respective walks with Christ. An example of this is when sports in your life begin to take away from time that you need to be devoting to God.

Paul tells us in 1 Corinthians 9:27 that he trains spiritually so that he does not become disqualified for the prize. If a person comes into a game when he hasn't been practicing or is out of shape, he is not qualified to play. He will not reach his potential.

The same is true in our spiritual lives: We need to continually bring ourselves under God's command so that we remain qualified for what He has for us. We need to be like Paul and press on toward the prize. —*Jay Beard*

Go

1. Are there any sins in your life that you realize you need to remove?

2. Are there any other hindrances in your spiritual life that you need to get rid of?
3. Are you continually keeping yourself under God's command so that you can stay focused on the prize?

Workout
Hebrews 12:1-3

Overtime
God, I want to win the prize. Please show me the areas in my life where I need to train harder. Open my heart to the teaching of Your Holy Spirit. Amen.

Most Powerful Tool

Ready
All Scripture is inspired by God and is profitable for teaching, for rebuking, for correcting, for training in righteousness, so that the man of God may be complete, equipped for every good work.

2 TIMOTHY 3:16-17

Set
What is your most powerful athletic tool? Maybe it's the strength of your bench press. It might be the drive from your leg squats. Or is it the speed you have from all the agility training? These all are important, but I think that the most powerful tool in most sports today is simply the ball.

Think about it. Who is the most dangerous person in basketball? The man with the ball. You need the ball to do what it takes to win: score! Without the ball, Tiger Woods is just Eldrick, Michael Vick is just Mike, and the Rocket Clemens is just Roger. It is what these men do with the powerful tool—the ball—that makes them champions.

So if the ball is the most powerful tool in sport, what is the most powerful tool in life? Let's not speculate but just get right to it—it's God's Word, the Bible.

In his second letter to Timothy, Paul shows us what this means. God's Word teaches us many things. It teaches us what is right, what is wrong, helps us get it right and prepares us to keep it right in our lives. I can't think of any other tool in life that can do all that. The Bible can save us, free us, change us, protect us and make us what we are meant to be: children of Christ.

In most sports, without the ball, the game could not be what it is intended to be. In your life with Christ, without His Word, you cannot be what you are intended to be. God's Word is the tool that can fully equip and empower you to be all that God created you to be. In the same way that football without the ball is not football, the Christian life without God's Word is not truly a Christian life.
—*Jere Johnson*

Go
1. Do you consider the Bible to be a powerful tool or just a book you carry on Sundays?
2. How often do you use the Bible—the most powerful tool you own?
3. Today, how can you begin to use God's Word to bring greater meaning and purpose to your life?

Workout
Deuteronomy 8:3; Ephesians 6:10-17; Hebrews 4:12

Overtime
God, I want my most powerful tool to be the Bible. Ephesians 6:17 states that the sword of the Spirit is the Word of God. Write this on my heart and teach me how to use this sword so that I will be equipped for anything that might come my way. Amen.

Grieving with Hope

Brothers, we do not want you to be ignorant about those who fall asleep, or to grieve like the rest of men, who have no hope.

1 THESSALONIANS 4:13, *NIV*

Set

How do you go on after experiencing the unexpected death of a friend and loved one? The Illinois Wesleyan University football team was faced with this difficult task after the death of 21-year-old offensive lineman and cocaptain, Doug Schmied. Schmied passed away on August 24, 2005, after suffering complications from heatstroke. "This is a devastating loss for everyone who knew Doug," said Illinois Wesleyan head football coach Norm Eash.[11]

The Christians in Thessalonica were eagerly anticipating the return of the Lord Jesus. However, when fellow believers died and Christ had not returned yet, they began to fear that those believers would miss His return. In 1 Thessalonians, Paul assures them and us that we will one day be united with our brothers and sisters in Christ when He returns. He doesn't tell us not to grieve when a brother or sister in Christ passes on; he just encourages us to grieve with hope, knowing we will see them again.

The greatest decision that you or I will ever make (or not make) is to receive Jesus Christ into our lives. We may make many important decisions over our lifetime, but no other decision will have the same ramifications. This choice will either make or break your eternity. *—Josh Carter*

Go

1. How have you responded to the loss of someone close to you?
2. How can Paul's words encourage you when it comes to dealing with death?

3. How prepared are you for Christ's return?

Workout
Philippians 1:21-23; 1 Thessalonians 4:16-18; 2 Timothy 4:7-8

Overtime
*God, dealing with death is unavoidable. I thank You for the hope
You have given me through Your Son, Jesus Christ. Create in me an
urgency to share about Jesus' sacrifice and the eternal life secured
through His death and resurrection so that I can see my close
friends and family in heaven one day. Amen.*

The Word

Ready
The tempter came to him and said, "If You are the
Son of God, tell these stones to become bread."
Jesus answered, "It is written: 'Man does not live
on bread alone, but on every word that comes
from the mouth of God'."

MATTHEW 4:3-4, *NIV*

Set
Throughout my years of training as a wheelchair athlete, I have
found that memorizing and reciting Bible verses helps me in many
ways. It helps me to stay focused, to get to sleep and to stay calm in
anxious moments.

Prior to a race, I often recite a verse in my mind to calm my heart.
I know that God is going with me as I race and that He will give me
what I need on that particular day.

One of my strengths as a wheelchair racer is my endurance, but
I'm usually slow off the start. I will never forget the time when one of

my coaches shouted at me after a race about my slow start. "What were you thinking? Where was your mind, anyway?" she asked.

I didn't tell her that my thoughts were fixed on God and His Word, which gave me power that day. His Word continues to give me that same power every day as I compete and strive to live up to my highest potential. —*Judy Siegle*

Go

1. Where is your mind before competition? During competition? After the competition is over?
2. In what way could God's Word play a bigger part in your competition and in your life?
3. What are the distractions in your life that make it difficult for you to focus on His Word?

Workout

Proverbs 30:5; 1 Corinthians 1:25; Ephesians 6:10-18

Overtime

Father, help me to realize the importance of Your Word. Let my mind retain what I read so that I may carry Your wisdom in my heart and apply it to each new situation.

"How can a young man keep his way pure? By keeping Your word.

I have sought You with all my heart; don't let me wander from Your commands.

I have treasured Your word in my heart so that I may not sin against You.

Lord, may You be praised; teach me Your statutes"
(Psalm 119:9-12).

Whose Side?

Ready

When Joshua was near Jericho, he looked
up and saw a man standing in front of him with
a drawn sword in His hand. Joshua approached
Him and asked, "Are You for us or for our enemies?"
"Neither," He replied. "I have now come as
commander of the Lord's army."

JOSHUA 5:13-14

Set

After playing in and coaching thousands of games, I have found that I struggle with one main issue: Whose team is God on—my team or the other team? How can God pick sides? If He does pick sides, how does He decide which side to be on? If there are Christians on both teams, then how can God be on both teams? These questions challenge us as athletes and coaches.

Let me be honest with you. When I compete, I want God to be solely on my team and not on the other team! However, when we have that mind-set, we have it all wrong. In the Bible, Joshua was the commander of Israel's army and was preparing his troops for battle against Jericho when the commander of the Lord's army appeared to him. When Joshua asked him whose side he was on, the commander of the Lord's army replied, "Neither."

Does this mean that God doesn't take sides? Well, there is a bigger issue here. It's not whether the Lord is on our team or their team; it's whether or not we are on God's team! When we compete, we need to first recognize that we are on Team Jesus Christ, not the other way around. It is human nature to want God to stand on our sideline. However, God wants us to be on His side only! —*Dan Britton*

Go

1. How can you apply the concept of being on God's team (not God being on your team) the next time you compete or practice?

2. What impact could this make on your team if all of your teammates understood this concept?
3. Why is it so difficult for us to remember that God's team is the only team that matters?

Workout
Ephesians 5:1-10

Overtime
Lord, help me to compete knowing that I am on Your team and to remember that it's not about You being on my team. Give me the proper mind-set to play for You. Every time I step onto the field of competition, I will wear Your uniform.

What Are You?

Ready
Summoning the crowd along with His disciples, He said to them, "If anyone wants to be My follower, he must deny himself, take up his cross, and follow Me."
MARK 8:34

Set
One of the common questions posed to sports fans is, "Who do you follow?" Most people answer with a city, school or mascot: "I'm a Denver fan." "I follow the University of North Carolina." "I'm a Hoosier." No matter how you phrase it, we all follow one team or another. This applies to our lives in Christ as well.

It is not uncommon today to hear believers ask, "What are you?" Some say, "I am a Baptist." Others claim to be Methodist, Lutheran, Catholic and so on.

This has always disturbed me. I am proud of my Christian upbringing and the denominational truths that I have learned over the years, but when I accepted Jesus Christ as Lord and Savior of my life, I committed to Him. I didn't commit to some set of religious traditions or legalistic dos and don'ts.

In the Team FCA Competitor's Creed, I read, "I am a Christian first and last . . ." So when people ask me today what I am spiritually, I simply tell them that I am a Christian who happens to attend a Bible church. Jesus Christ is Who we are and should be. I am His!

Please do not misunderstand; I am not bashing your denominational preference. But do understand that the denomination in which you have been raised is nothing without the relationship you can have—and need to have—with Jesus Christ.

If you want to get caught up in anything, get caught up in the doctrine of Jesus Christ and His Word. To find out more, go to your Bible and begin to read more about Him!

So . . . What are you? As for me and my household, we tell others, "I am a Christian first and last!" I hope you can say that, too! —*Jere Johnson*

Go

1. Who or what do you follow?
2. Are you caught up in the dos and don'ts of your faith, or are you caught up in Jesus Christ?
3. Do you know how to begin being who you really are in Him? (If not, please let us know! We will always point you to the cross of Christ!)

Workout
Joshua 24:15; Psalms 111:9-11; John 14:6

Overtime
Father, thank You for Your Son. Help me today to find my identity solely in Him.

Ready

Do you not know that your body is a temple of the Holy Spirit, who is in you, whom you have received from God?

1 CORINTHIANS 6:19, *NIV*

Set

The question for any athlete to consider is, "What does God think about my sex life?" After all, it is to the heavenly Umpire that we must one day give an account!

God is not a Cosmic Killjoy. He wants us to enjoy life. He wants us to have a great sex life! But the Creator knows and has told us the time and place for everything. Sexual relations with a permanent spouse is God's plan. He tells us, "It is God's will that you should be sanctified [set apart to Him]; that you should avoid sexual immorality; that each of you should learn to control his own body in a way that is holy and honorable" (1 Thessalonians 4:3-4, *NIV*).

As athletes, most of us consider ourselves to be independent, self-sufficient and able to handle anything. But 1 Corinthians 10:12 says, "So, if you think you are standing firm, be careful that you don't fall!" (*NIV*). We are really not as strong as we think!

Frankly, the majority of movies, television shows and secular videos are trash. The world's music is full of suggestive lyrics that influence listeners. Spiritually, the mind that dwells on impure thoughts soon begins to rationalize, compromise and finally lose control. As Christian athletes, we must control our minds and replace any impure thoughts with thoughts of things that are pure.
—*Elliot Johnson*

Go

1. As an athlete, what sexual pressures do you face? How are you tempted by what you see, hear, talk about or do?
2. How might giving in to sexual pressure distract you from your game?

3. What will you choose to do when tempted?

Workout
1 Corinthians 6:18; 2 Timothy 2:22; 1 Peter 2:11; 1 John 1:9

Overtime
Father, I am bombarded each day with outside influences that encourage me to do things that do not honor You. I realize that sexual purity requires more than just abstaining from sex—it requires that I guard my mind as well as my actions. Grow in me a discernment and strength to turn away from things that cause me to stray from a standard of purity that brings You honor. Amen.

Brothers and Sisters

Ready
Therefore, be imitators of God, as dearly loved children. And walk in love, as the Messiah also loved us and gave Himself for us, a sacrificial and fragrant offering to God.
EPHESIANS 5:1-2

Set
Speed skater Kristen Talbot made headlines in 1992 when she gave up her Olympic dreams to donate bone marrow to her critically ill brother. Talbot proved that she wanted to keep her brother in her life and was committed to doing everything she could to support him during his physical illness, even at the expense of the hard work and practice she had put in on the ice over the years. She demonstrated extreme personal sacrifice to benefit someone she loved.

Often we take our brothers and sisters for granted. We do not carve out time from our schedule to spend with them. We don't invite them to join us in activities. We don't ask about their days or show interest in their lives.

In Ephesians 5:1-2 the apostle Paul tells us to "walk in love, as the Messiah also loved us and gave Himself for us." Consider ways that you can live out Paul's instruction by serving your family members.

For example, you might want to surprise your brothers or sisters by doing their chores for them. Take the time to listen to them instead of ignoring what they say. Invite them to join you and your friends for an activity. Ask forgiveness for times when you treated them unkindly or spoke harsh words to them.

As you give up something for a family member, think about what Jesus Christ gave up for you: His life. And in doing so, He made it possible for you to experience ultimate forgiveness and a personal relationship with God for eternity. —*Roxanne Robbins*

Go

1. How do you treat your brothers and sisters? How do you treat the rest of your family members?
2. Today, how can you show them that you love them based on the example of Christ's love for us?
3. How does this lesson apply to the rest of your brothers and sisters in Christ?

Workout
1 Peter 3:8-9; 1 John 3:11-24

Overtime
Jesus, I don't say it enough, but thank You for Your sacrifice on the cross. All of Your actions were done out of love. Please help me demonstrate that love with my own actions. Help me appreciate my friends and family whom You have placed in my life, and show me how I can serve them in love. Don't let me take them for granted. Amen.

Ready

Do you not know that your body is a sanctuary of the
Holy Spirit who is in you, whom you have from God?
You are not your own, for you were bought at a price;
therefore glorify God in your body.

1 CORINTHIANS 6:19-20

Set

When the NFL's Baltimore Ravens are getting ready to go into battle, the sound system blasts music and the giant screens exhort the team to "Protect this House." This same scene is replayed week after week in stadiums all around the league. In the history of sports, there has never been a team that has liked losing on their home field. That is why most homecoming games are scheduled against competition that the home team should easily defeat.

God refers to our bodies as His house. Because we are believers, the Holy Spirit actually lives inside of us. And because God lives within us, He expects us to protect His house! This is a high standard, especially since we live in a culture that promotes winning above all else.

Because the pressure to win is so great, many athletes have resorted to trying just about anything that will take their game to the next level. Each year, hundreds of athletes test positive for illegal or banned substances. Performance-enhancing drug use has become so prevalent that each major sport has established elaborate drug-testing policies with increasing penalties for offenders.

God calls us to a different standard. He does not want us to do anything that would cause harm to our bodies or bring dishonor to His name. The reputation of athletes who test positive for drug use is forever tarnished. For believers, the name and reputation of Jesus also will be harmed. When we resort to banned or illegal substances to improve our performance, we are basically putting our trust and confidence in those substances. We are saying that the power of God is not able to give us the discipline, the determination, the drive or the talent to compete at our best. —*Jimmy Page*

Go

1. What substances do you put in your body that might bring dishonor to the name of Christ?
2. What would Jesus think about what you are willing to do in order to succeed in your sport?
3. Are you willing to stop using any questionable substances or supplements today?

Workout

Romans 8:9-11; Philippians 1:20-21; 2 Timothy 1:7

Overtime

Lord, help me to realize that Your Holy Spirit lives in me. Help me to protect Your house from anything that is harmful to my body or that dishonors Your name.

Right or Left?

Ready

But a man named Ananias, with Sapphira his wife, sold a piece of property. However, he kept back part of the proceeds with his wife's knowledge, and brought a portion of it and laid it at the apostles' feet. Then Peter said, "Ananias, why has Satan filled your heart to lie to the Holy Spirit and keep back part of the proceeds from the field?"

ACTS 5:1-3

Set

When I played little league football for the Sharks, we had an undefeated season. We were so good that not a single team even scored against us. Not bad for eight-year-olds!

Needless to say, teams feared the Sharks. After our games, Coach Buckley would hand out the coveted "110%" helmet stickers to players who had played with all their heart and had given that extra effort on the field.

As competitors, we can sometimes be tempted to hold back what is God's for our own pleasure. But God wants us to give Him what is right, not what's left. In Luke 6:38, Jesus says:

Give, and it will be given to you; a good measure, pressed down, shaken together, and running over will be poured into your lap. For with the measure that you use, it will be measured back to you.

Ananias gave what was left, not what was right. Abel gave what was right; Cain gave what was left. We have the choice every time we step onto the field: give what is right or give what's left. Most athletes give God the leftovers and keep the best for themselves.

God is not honored by our leftovers. The challenge when competing is to release all of your talents, gifts and abilities to become more like Christ on and off the field. We cannot hold back or keep some for ourselves. —*Dan Britton*

Go

1. What does it mean to give God what is right instead of what is left?
2. When is it hard to give God what is right? On the field? Off the field? During practice? During games?
3. How can you make sure that you always give God what is right?

Workout
Leviticus 23:10; 1 Timothy 6:7-9

Overtime
Lord, I know You desire for me to give You all my talents
for Your glory. It is hard to totally release all my abilities for You.
My selfish desires often want the glory. I confess my sin.
Please, Lord, renew my mind. Help me to give You 100 percent
of the glory when I compete.

Ready

I am sure of this, that He who started a
good work in you will carry it on to completion
until the day of Christ Jesus.

PHILIPPIANS 1:6

Set

At the college that I attended, we referred to long-distance runners as
"jar heads." We figured that each day they would unscrew their
heads, take out their brains, and then run an unbelievable amount of
miles before returning and putting their brains back in their heads.

I say this all in good fun, obviously. I have always admired distance runners and think that distance running is an amazing ability.
When these runners race, they set their minds on finishing the race.
Lap after lap they strain through sore muscles and tough conditions
to finish what they started.

In a way, you could say that we're all distance runners. When
we're born, our race begins—the race of life. There may be no ribbons
or trophies in our life's race, but there can be an amazing prize. Jesus
Christ will one day return. At the finish line, Christ Himself will be
waiting to congratulate those whom He recognizes.

If you believe in Him and He has found residence in your heart
and life, you will receive the prize of heaven. But if you have lived for
yourself and have denied Him through sinful choices, when you
cross over the finish line, you will be finished. He will not know you,
for you did not desire to know Him when you had the chance. We all
will cross the finish line one day. Will the results of your efforts
result in His glory?

Give your all for God all of the time, while you still have the
opportunity. Never give up, give out, or give in to what the world
holds on to today. You are a warrior. Compete for Him, run for Him,
and run to Him daily. Finally, be confident in this: If you belong to
Him, He will complete the work in you at the finish line! Keep up
your endurance. One day it will all be worth it! —*Jere Johnson*

Go

1. How are you running your race?
2. Are you running as a member of His team, or are you running for yourself?
3. How can you start to be a road warrior for Him today?

Workout

Psalm 64; Matthew 5:12; 1 Corinthians 1:8

Overtime

Lord, as I live my life for You today, help me run with endurance to the finish line that You have marked for me. Only You know when my time on Earth is to come to an end. Help me run for You and only You until that day. I am Yours, Lord—all of me for all of You! Until the end, amen.

One Thing

Ready

Brothers, I do not consider myself to have taken hold of it. But one thing I do: forgetting what is behind and reaching forward to what is ahead, I pursue as my goal the prize promised by God's heavenly call in Christ Jesus.

PHILIPPIANS 3:13-14

Set

Paul uses the phrase "one thing" to bring focus and clarity to his calling. This phrase appears five times in the *New International Version* of the Bible—once in the verse above in Philippians and four times in the Gospels:

- In Luke 10:42, Jesus says to Martha, "only one thing is needed."
- In both Luke 18:22 and Mark 10:21, Jesus tells the rich man that he still lacks "one thing."

- In John 9:25, the blind man who was healed by Christ tells the Pharisees, "One thing I do know. I was blind but now I see!"

As competitors for Christ, the one thing that God desires is for us to focus on Him. The FCA Competitor's Creed states: "I am a Competitor now and forever. I am made to strive, to strain, to stretch and to succeed in the arena of competition. I am a Christian Competitor and as such, I face my challenger with the face of Christ."

The one thing that we need to focus on as competitors for Christ is the fact that we have been created in the likeness of God Almighty in order to bring glory to Him on and off the field. Period. Anything else takes our focus off the Master. —*Dan Britton*

Go

1. As a competitor, what makes it hard for you to keep your focus?
2. As you examine your walk with the Lord, what is one thing that prevents you from keeping your focus on the Lord?
3. What would you describe as the one thing on which the Lord wants you to focus?

Workout
Luke 10:38-42; 18:18-30; John 9:13-34

Overtime
Lord, there are so many things that take my focus off of You. Please forgive me for those times when I have not fixed my eyes on You. Help me, Lord, to focus on You alone when I compete. I desire to glorify You in all that I do.

Damaging Words

Ready

So also, the tongue is a small thing, but what enormous damage it can do.

JAMES 3:5, *NLT*

Set

Foul language, swearing and cuss words are commonplace in athletics today. Some say these words motivate players. Others say that they are necessary to get the point or lesson across. But if this is the case, how do teachers and preachers teach lessons of life without using these words? If this type of language is used to motivate, why is over 90 percent of it used in a negative context?

In the New Testament, James shares that the tongue (our words) is a very dangerous weapon. Controlling our speech is vitally important in our spiritual journey. Often we are judged not by what we do but by what comes out of our mouth.

Coach John Wooden was as successful as any coach, but he did not have to use foul language in order to coach his team. Many coaches have had great success without resorting to such language. To them, I am sure that controlling the tongue also meant controlling other areas in their coaching (such as anger and attitude).

Many athletes say that swearing is a habit that is hard to break. However, just like the skills in a sport, guarding your tongue is a discipline that needs to be practiced. Have you considered the damage that your words do to your teammates? Think about what would happen if you stopped swearing today and used different words to convey your message. Want better morale on your team? Clean up the talk and see what happens.

If you don't swear, good for you, but let your teammates know that swearing bothers you as well. Raise the standard of your program by raising the expectations for the kind of language used by staff and athletes alike. I guarantee that you will see the difference.
—*Jere Johnson*

1. When do you struggle with foul language?
2. When your language goes south, what comes along for the ride? Your anger? Your attitude?
3. Today, how can you start to tame your tongue and use words that will not offend others around you?

Workout
Matthew 5:37; James 3:1-12

Overtime
Jesus, my tongue needs to be controlled by You. I pray that my words will encourage others and that I will be an athlete who is known for using my speech to lift up those around me.

What Do You Sow?

Ready
A man reaps what he sows. The one who sows to please his sinful nature, from that nature will reap destruction; the one who sows to please the Spirit, from the Spirit will reap eternal life.

GALATIANS 6:7-8, *NIV*

Set
After injuries to ligaments in both knees cut his 2001 and 2002 seasons short, Oklahoma quarterback Jason White wanted desperately to get back on the field with his teammates. "For a while, it didn't seem like it would happen," White said.

White not only got back on the field in 2003, but he also led the Sooners to a 12-1 record and won the Heisman Trophy, the highest honor in college football. When reflecting on the grueling rehab that he had gone through to get to this point, White said, "I'd go through it all again."[12]

God's principle of reaping what we sow is often very evident in athletics. Those who sow the seeds of hard work and mental preparation will generally reap a harvest of success in competition. Those who sow seeds of physical and mental laziness will reap a harvest of disappointment.

There are two main things that we must remember about a harvest. First, the harvest is always in the future. We must sow seeds before we can reap. Second, it is always based upon what was sown. If a farmer sows corn, he will reap a harvest of corn. In Galatians 6:8, Paul states:

> The one who sows to please his sinful nature, from that nature will reap destruction; the one who sows to please the Spirit, from the Spirit will reap eternal life.

You are going to sow many seeds today, and at some point you will reap a harvest according to what was sown. The key is to first know what kind of harvest you want to reap and then sow the seeds that will produce it. I challenge you today to sow seeds in competition and in life that bring glory and honor to God, and know that you will be rewarded with a great harvest. —*Josh Carter*

Go

1. What is the greatest harvest you have ever reaped in athletics?
2. What seeds were sown to bring this harvest?
3. What kind of harvest do you want to reap in life? Are you sowing seeds that will produce it?

Workout
Proverbs 11:18; 22:8; Hosea 10:12-13; Romans 6:21-22

Overtime
Father, help me to sow life and not death. I want to reap a good, bountiful harvest, and I know that this will be accomplished only when I allow You to have complete control in my life. I pray that each seed I plant will be pleasing to You.

Ready

Walk as children of light—for the fruit of the light results in all goodness, righteousness, and truth—discerning what is pleasing to the Lord.

EPHESIANS 5:8-10

Set

If someone walked up to you and asked, "What does it mean to play 'in the zone'?" how would you respond? What professional athlete comes to your mind when you think about playing in the zone? As an athlete, you have certainly been in the zone at least once. To play in the zone means that you are unstoppable. You are the "go to." You can't miss. I think you get the point—when you are in the zone, it is an awesome experience.

What does in the zone mean if you relate it to your spiritual life instead of your sports experience? Have you ever been in the zone spiritually? What does it take to get in the zone? Let's dig deeper with a few questions based on Ephesians 5:1-10.

- Who in the Bible lived "in the zone"? Why?
- Paul says to be an imitator of God (see v. 1). What does it mean to imitate someone?
- What things does Paul say someone should do to imitate God (see vv. 3-7)?
- When playing in the zone, an athlete is unstoppable. When you are living in the zone for Christ, what does your life look like (see vv. 8-10)?

The 1924 Olympic runner Eric Liddell said, "God made me fast. And when I run, I feel God's pleasure. To win is to honor Him." Ask God to show you what it means to play in the zone for Christ. Pray that you will discover more ways to please Him and not please yourself. The FCA Competitor's Creed states: "I give my all—all of the time." When you're giving your all for Christ, you can bet that you're spiritually in the zone.
—*Dan Britton*

Go

1. When you compete, whom do you try to please?
2. What can you do to please God during competition?
3. How do you sense God's pleasure when you compete?

Workout
3 John 1:11

Overtime

Lord, I am consumed with my own performance.
Break me of the hold that competition has on me. My prayer is
that all who see me compete will know that it is all about You.
Transform me into Your agent of change.

Etc.

Ready

Though we live in the world, we do not wage war
as the world does. The weapons we fight with
are not the weapons of the world. On the contrary,
they have divine power to demolish strongholds.
We demolish arguments and every pretension
that sets itself up against the knowledge of God,
and we take captive every thought to make it
obedient to Christ.

2 CORINTHIANS 10:3-5, *NIV*

Set

As a competitor, I constantly struggle with my thoughts. I have
thoughts of doubt, confusion and pride, just to name a few. I wrestle
with doubting my athletic ability and potential, my place on the
team, and my acceptance from teammates. It is usually my mind that
is the greatest challenge, not my physical ability. My mind runs wild
with speculation.

My college lacrosse coach would always post his daily practice plan before practice began. Based on where he would put my name on the practice plan, I would think better or worse of my ability. My thoughts would race as to why my coach had listed me in the order that he did, thinking that he had either moved me up or down in the rotation. I later found out that he had no real reason for moving the names around.

As a competitor, you need to take every thought captive. If you abbreviate "every thought captive," you get "etc." What a great reminder from the Lord! Surrender every thought and make it obedient to Christ.

This is one of the toughest challenges for a Christian competitor. It is a daily battle not to let your mind run with incorrect thoughts. Every stray thought needs to be submitted to the Lord. Don't let others control your mind—only Christ. —*Dan Britton*

Go

1. When it comes to competition, what kind of thoughts do you battle?
2. Why does Christ want you to take every thought that you have captive?
3. How can you apply the "etc." principle to your competition (for example, writing "etc." on your shoe or posting it in your locker)?

Workout
Colossians 3:1-4

Overtime
Lord, I need Your help. My thoughts often plague me.
Free me from thoughts of doubt and pride, for these are not of You.
I desire to take every thought captive! When I compete,
let Your thoughts be my thoughts.

The No-Look Pass

Ready

For I am convinced that neither death nor life . . . nor anything else in all creation, will be able to separate us from the love of God that is in Christ Jesus our Lord.

ROMANS 8:38-39, *NIV*

Set

Mike is one of my best friends. He is a natural-born athlete, while I, on the other hand, am a natural-born glutton for punishment. When Mike and I were in college and graduate school, we spent a lot of time working at our neighborhood pool during the summers. When there was a break in the action, we'd play some basketball on one of the courts that were adjacent to the pool. I never beat him head-to-head. Let's just say that he was the Kevin McHale of our neighborhood, while I played basketball like the swimmer I was.

However, sometimes one of Mike's friends from college, Jeff, would stop by for a visit, and Mike would let me play on the same side with him and Jeff. Notwithstanding my participation, we were unstoppable. No matter who we played or what defense they threw at us, Mike and Jeff had an unnatural ability to find each other on the court and make the winning play. All I needed to do was to set the occasional pick and pull down the occasional rebound. They did the rest. No-look passes. Give-and-gos. You name it, they executed it, often without so much as exchanging a look or a word. They had the ultimate in-game level of trust in one another.

When hard times come along, it can be difficult to trust God's plan for our lives. When it comes to trusting God, it is a lot like those no-look passes that Mike and Jeff used to dish out on the basketball court. There is not a method or process for trust that we need to learn; we simply need to accept that God is not going to let us down when it comes to the truly important things in our lives. After all, nothing can separate us from God's love for us. —*Stan Smith*

1. Why is it hard to trust that Jesus will help you win your battles?
2. What prevents you from trusting in His plan for your life?
3. Can you focus on the strength that Jesus gives you to serve Him?

Workout

2 Kings 6:8-23; Mark 9:14-25; James 1:5-8

Overtime

Lord, thank You for Your constant protection in our lives and faithful guidance in our roles as spiritual leaders on our teams and in our schools and homes. Help us to finish the work You have laid out for each of us. Amen.

The Lord's Army

Ready

But if it doesn't please you to worship the Lord, choose for yourselves today the one you will worship: the gods your fathers worshiped beyond the Euphrates River, or the gods of the Amorites in whose land you are living. As for me and my family, we will worship the Lord.

JOSHUA 24:15

Set

I was at home one morning, just minding my own business, when I heard a proclamation coming from outside of my house. It was loud. It was proud. It was my four-year-old son singing at the top of his voice, "I'm in the Lord's Army. *Yes, sir!*" He was sitting against the door with his lightsaber in hand, singing his praise to the General of the heavenly Host.

When you play sports, you enter into battle. Sides are chosen, boundaries are drawn, and the battle begins. No matter what the sport, you choose whom you will compete for and against. This is no different from your walk with Christ.

Every day you battle against the evil of the world. You are in a war for your soul. The battle began the minute you were born! And today, God wants you to choose whose army you will fight for.

Evan, my son, had made his choice. He was loud and he was proud. He didn't care if the neighbors heard him singing boldly about his allegiance. What about you? Can you say the same today?

Whether you believe it or not, you are in a spiritual army. If you are not with Christ, then you are against Him. It is that simple. Every day when you wake up, you must choose whom you will serve during that day. Strive every day to serve Christ.

Satan is out to destroy our land and everyone in it. Get with the program, and sign up for active duty! Sing loud and proud that you, this day, are in the Lord's Army! —*Jere Johnson*

Go

1. Can you proudly state today that you are fighting for the Lord's Army? Why or why not?
2. Are you staying well equipped to fend off Satan's attacks? If not, how could you be better equipped?
3. How can you start your active-duty service today in the Lord's Army?

Workout
Deuteronomy 30:16-18; Romans 8:37-38; Ephesians 6:12

Overtime
God, I want to fight on Your side. Help me be confident in my decision to live my life for You. I pray that Your Holy Spirit will teach me how I can be equipped to fight the battle against Satan and his evil schemes. Today, I choose to worship You, Lord. Amen.

Ready

Do nothing out of selfish ambition or vain conceit, but in humility consider others better than yourselves. Each of you should look not only to your own interests, but also to the interests of others.

PHILIPPIANS 2:3-4, *NIV*

Set

Touchdown celebrations have reached a whole new level these days. High-fives from your teammates just don't cut it anymore. After making a touchdown catch against the Giants in week 15 of the 2003 season, New Orleans Saints' wide receiver Joe Horn pulled out his cell phone from the goalpost and made a call from the end zone. One NFL coach responded, "This is a team game. There was a quarterback that threw the ball, and there was an offensive line that protected for him. I just think that when you draw attention to yourself, it's not necessary."[13]

A friend of mine had "TLINAU" put on his license plates. One day my curiosity got the better of me, so I asked him what the letters meant. "This life is not about us," he replied. I was intrigued by the message as I thought about how often I selfishly live my life as if the world *does* revolve around me. Oh, of course, I would never say that it does, but don't we often do things in a way that says "It's all about me"?

In the sports world, it's important to remember that purposely drawing attention to yourself minimizes the efforts of the rest of the team. It's selfish and arrogant, and such showboating drives a stake between you and your teammates. Jesus Christ came to Earth to carry out the will of God for the benefit of others and to give up His life so that others could live. He was all about serving other people through love. He did nothing out of selfish ambition. May we follow His example and remember that this life is not about us but about serving God and serving others. —*Josh Carter*

1. What is something you have done to draw attention to yourself in competition?
2. Why should you honor your team above yourself?
3. What can you do today to take the focus off yourself?

Workout
Matthew 20:28; Romans 12:3,10,16; Philippians 2:4-7

Overtime
Father, I realize that many times the motivation behind my actions is not honorable. Please teach me how to put others' needs before my own, for this life is not about me.

The Flying Scotsman

Ready
You did not choose Me, but I chose you. I appointed you that you should go out and produce fruit, and that your fruit should remain, so that whatever you ask the Father in My name, He will give you.

JOHN 15:16

Set
Known as the Flying Scotsman, Eric Liddell ran to victory in the 1924 Paris Olympics. He won a gold medal in the 400-meter dash and set a new world record with his time of 47.6 seconds.

Liddell ran, spoke and lived his life with incredible faithfulness. He never wavered from his commitment to Jesus Christ. The classic movie *Chariots of Fire* shows just how much of an impact Liddell made by living out his convictions.

Liddell was not well-known or popular—just faithful. He was known as the one who always shook the hands of other runners before each race. At the time, the runners ran on cinder tracks, and

Liddell would offer his trowel (small shovel) to fellow runners who had trouble digging their starting holes.

Even though Liddell was known as the Flying Scotsman, he just as easily could have been called the Serving Scotsman. God used him in a significant way because he was willing to take his eyes off of himself and focus on those around him.

As an athlete, it is hard to intentionally serve others, especially in the heat of competition. But remember that God has "appointed you that you should go out and produce fruit, and that your fruit should remain." To honor God is to serve Him in all we do, and serving Him means total victory! —*Dan Britton*

Go

1. What kind of athlete are you in the heat of competition? Are you so focused on winning that you do not see the ways that God could use you to serve others?
2. What are some practical ways that you can serve athletes around you?
3. What "fruit" can God produce if you focus on serving others? What changes can God bring about in your own life if you take on this kind of service-oriented mind-set?

Workout
John 13; Philippians 2:1-11

Overtime
Lord, help me to be an athlete who cares about those whom I compete against. Show me practical ways to serve them. I ask for a servant's heart, Lord. May my talents and abilities be used for Your service. Amen.

Measuring the Heart

Ready
Man does not see what the Lord sees, for man sees what is visible, but the Lord sees the heart.

1 SAMUEL 16:7

Set
Another signing day has passed in college football. The rankings are out and once again colleges like USC, Oklahoma, Florida State and Michigan have locked down the best high school athletes in the country. "Blue chippers," high school All-Americans and All-Stars have made their decisions, and now coaches and fans will begin to celebrate their recruiting victories.

These players are amazing physical specimens in every way. Offensive linemen come in weighing over 300 pounds, wide receivers and defensive backs run the 40-meter in under 4.4 seconds, and quarterbacks are 6' 5" and can throw the football 80 yards on the fly. But even with all these gifts and abilities, there is no guarantee that these players will succeed. No system exists that can successfully measure the athlete's "heart." Teams must have true heart in order to be successful, but this is difficult to find.

God values our heart above our outward appearance or abilities. In 1 Samuel 16:1-13, Saul, having lost favor with God, was rejected as king. So the prophet Samuel was sent to the home of Jesse to anoint one of Jesse's sons as the next king of Israel. Jesse was sure that Eliab, his eldest, would be chosen, but he was not God's choice. Meanwhile, David, the youngest, was out tending sheep. He was so far from the action that his father hadn't even considered him for the job. But God knew David's heart and that he would do anything He asked.

Over the next four years, many of today's five-star talented athletes will fade. Recruits with less glamour but more heart will surface and become the better players. They will be willing to do whatever it takes to excel both individually and as part of a team. God is also in the recruiting business. Today, if you were to stand before Him as Jesse's sons did so long ago, would He choose you? —*Charles Gee*

Go

1. Why is true heart so difficult to measure?
2. Who are some players that you have known who have had only average physical skills but great heart?
3. How do you think God feels about a person who has captured His heart?

Workout
1 Samuel 16:1-13; Acts 13:20-22

Overtime
God, help me to not get distracted by what I see with my natural eyes. Help me to see what You see when it comes to the heart. Help my heart and my actions to be pure so that I can be used by You. Amen.

The Playbook

Ready
I have kept my feet from every evil path to follow Your word. I have not turned from Your judgments, for You Yourself have instructed me. How sweet Your word is to my taste—[sweeter] than honey to my mouth. I gain understanding from Your precepts; therefore I hate every false way. Your word is a lamp for my feet and a light on my path.

PSALM 119:101-105

Set
One of the common elements in all levels of football, from pee-wee to pro, is the playbook. It contains the game plan that each team uses to try to overcome its opponent. Without the playbook, teams and players would be in a state of confusion, not knowing what to do or where to go. On the other hand, no matter how good the playbook is, it's absolutely useless if the players don't study it and apply it on the field.

When it comes to life, there is no better playbook than the Word of God. It contains everything we need to defeat the opposition (the devil). Although we may recognize that God has a plan for our lives, we often do not acknowledge that the devil also has a game plan for our lives, which is in complete opposition to God's.

The devil's plan is to steal and kill and destroy our lives, while God's plan is to give us a full and abundant life. "A thief comes only to steal and to kill and to destroy. I have come that they may have life and have it in abundance" (John 10:10).

In order for us to consistently overcome our life's adversary, we must (1) know what God's "playbook" says by reading and studying it, and (2) apply what it says to our lives. If we don't, we are playing right into the hands of our enemy.

I encourage you to study and apply God's "playbook"—the Bible—to your life this week so that you can avoid being sacked by the devil! —*Josh Carter*

Go

1. How has following your team's playbook or game plan affected your performance in competition?
2. How often do you turn to God's playbook—the Bible—for guidance?
3. What are some specific ways in which you can apply God's Word to your life today?

Workout
Matthew 7:24-27; Luke 11:28; James 1:19-25

Overtime
*God, thank You for providing us with a playbook for life—
the Holy Bible. I pray that as I spend time reading Your Word,
the promises in this playbook will be written on my heart.
Help me apply what I read in my day-to-day life.
Amen.*

Ready

Therefore, since we are surrounded by
such a great cloud of witnesses, let us throw
off everything that hinders and the sin that
so easily entangles, and let us run with perseverance
the race marked out for us.

HEBREWS 12:1, *NIV*

Set

Imagine this: You are on the field, the mat, the court or the track, and the stands are full of cheering spectators. The crowd is watching your every move. As athletes, we thrive under these circumstances.

But do we remember that every day, whether competing or not, we have heavenly and earthly witnesses watching our every move? We must realize that we don't compete or perform to please the crowds; rather, we should strive to please God alone. We should compete to show God's glory to those who are watching us.

Athletes know that it takes years of dedication and devotion to achieve excellence in their sport. They train every day to perfect their techniques and avoid all of those things that could hurt their performance. This is also true in our spiritual lives.

Daily, we need to set aside time with God to learn His ways so that we can show others His ways. We need to pray and ask God to help us stay away from all of the things that keep us from a closer relationship with Jesus. We need to ask Him to help us avoid those things that keep us from excelling in our sport.

We are an example to others of God's greatness and love. We have a lifetime commitment to training as an athlete both physically and spiritually, and this commitment holds great rewards.

Spectators are watching both in heaven and here on earth. Commit to showing them God's greatness and an athlete who loves the Lord. —*Kande Speers*

Go

1. What role do audiences play in your competition?
2. How are you showing them God's greatness and love?
3. What ways will you show God's glory to those watching?

Workout

1 Corinthians 9:24-25; Philippians 3:14; 1 Timothy 4:7-8;
Hebrews 2:1; 3:13

Overtime

God, help me to remain disciplined as I set aside time for You each day. Help me to retain and actively use what the Bible teaches me. I want each of my actions to show others Your perfect love. Amen.

Focus Factor

Ready

But my eyes [look] to You, Lord God. I seek refuge in You; do not let me die. Protect me from the trap they have set for me, and from the snares of evildoers. Let the wicked fall into their own nets, while I pass [safely] by.

PSALM 141:8-10

Set

"I was telling myself 20 times a hole (to) keep my focus, keep my focus, keep my focus," Michael Campbell said, "and it worked."[14] Michael Campbell began the final round of the 2005 U.S. Open at Pinehurst four shots behind the leader. However, he was one of only four golfers who shot under par on the final day, while those atop the leader board crumbled, giving him a two-shot victory over Tiger Woods.

Campbell's focus on the golf course paid off—to the tune of $1.17 million. "I worked really hard for this, ups and downs from my whole career," Campbell said. "But it's worth the work. It's just amazing."[15]

The word "focus" can be defined as "a state or condition permitting clear perception or understanding.[16] Whether it is sports or life that we are talking about, our ability to stay focused on the right things can dramatically affect the direction we go. If our desire is to compete for Christ, then our focus must be fixed squarely on Him in all aspects of competition. On the other hand, if our focus is not on Him, our competition is meaningless.

Today, may you be completely focused on Christ and on accomplishing His plan for you—both in and out of competition. —*Josh Carter*

Go

1. What causes you to lose focus during competition?
2. Where is your focus in life currently fixed? Is that where you want it to be?
3. Is it possible to be focused both on Christ and your sport? How?

Workout
Isaiah 46:8-13; Hebrews 3:1; 12:2

Overtime
Father, so often I put the focus on myself. I forget that everything I do should be for You alone. Help me to compete for You and have my eyes constantly set upward toward You.

"Let your eyes look forward;
fix your gaze straight ahead.

Carefully consider the path for your feet,
and all your ways will be established.

Don't turn to the right or to the left;
keep your feet away from evil"
(Proverbs 4:25-27).

The Competitor's Prayer

Ready

Pour out your hearts before Him. God is our refuge.

Set

Many times, pre-game prayers can be like a "rah-rah" talk or a desperate plea to God for a big win. But as true competitors, we need to ask, "What is the proper way to pray before entering the battle? How should we pour out our hearts before God so that we will be spiritually ready for competition?" Here is a great prayer that you can pray before a game, competition, workout or even practice:

"Lord, I compete for You alone. In every victory and every loss, I play for You. Every time I compete, I stand for the cross. My love for the game is evidence of my love for You. I play for You, Lord, when I put on the uniform, lace up the shoes and walk out of the locker room. I declare my loyalty to You.

"My drive comes from the Holy Spirit. Through the pain and through the cheers, I will not give in or give up. My passion for competition comes from above. I sweat for the One who made me. The champion inside of me is Jesus. My only goal is to glorify the name of Christ. To win is to honor Him.

"I feel Your delight when I compete. All of my abilities are from You, Jesus. My heart yearns for Your applause. I am under Your authority. I will respect and honor my teammates, coaches and opponents. I will play by the rules. I will submit to You as my Ultimate Coach.

"I am Your warrior in the heat of battle. I am humble in victory and gracious in defeat. I serve those on my team and those I compete against. My words inspire and motivate. I utter what You desire. My body is Your temple; nothing enters my body that is not honoring to You. I train to bring You glory. My sweat is an offering to my heavenly Master.

"I wear Your jersey, Lord. Victory does not lie in winning but in becoming more like You. There is no greater victory. In Your name, I pray. Amen." —*Dan Britton*

Go

1. What are your pre-game prayers like?
2. Do you define winning by the scoreboard or by Christlike competition?
3. How can you develop your prayer life in the arena of competition?

Workout

Mark 11:24-25; John 5:14-15

Overtime

Lord, I admit that my prayers before competition are more focused on the scoreboard than on becoming like You. I desire to pour out my heart before You every day that I compete. Develop in me a pure heart. Amen.

Surprising Strength

Ready

I have great confidence in you; I have great pride in you. I am filled with encouragement; I am overcome with joy in all our afflictions.

2 CORINTHIANS 7:4

Set

Have you ever been nervous before a big game? Have you ever felt like quitting an event before you even got started? The first time I competed in the Boston Marathon, I didn't think I belonged in the race. As I sat on the starting line, in my mind I was yelling at my coach, *I don't belong in this race! I'm not strong enough!*

However, one of the most amazing things happened to me that day. Although on the starting line I doubted my ability to even finish the famous Boston Marathon, 26 miles later I had won the race and broken the world record by almost seven minutes! I was stronger than I thought I was!

When the Israelites were preparing to enter the land of Canaan, they were most likely also a bit nervous. Moses had died and they were now under the leadership of Joshua. However, God told them to be strong and courageous, for He was about to give the land that He had promised to them. He said to Joshua:

I have given you every place where the sole of your foot treads, just as I promised Moses. Your territory will be from the wilderness and Lebanon to the great Euphrates River—all the land of the Hittites—and west to the Mediterranean Sea. No one will be able to stand against you as long as you live. I will be with you, just as I was with Moses. I will not leave you or forsake you (Joshua 1:3-5).

Being nervous before an event is normal. It tells us that what we're about to do is important. But God encourages us in the Bible to be brave and to take courage by performing for Him, the audience of One.

Don't allow those anxious feelings to keep you from challenging yourself. The outcome could surprise you! —*Jean Driscoll*

Go
1. Can you describe a time when you were anxious before a competition? Where was your focus? Were you able to overcome your anxiety?
2. What situations in competition typically make you anxious? If your approach to that situation was not anxious but courageous, on what would you be focusing?
3. Off the track, do you seek the Lord's strength to help you overcome little worries that plague your day?

Workout
Joshua 1:9; 2 Samuel 22:33; Ephesians 3:20; Philippians 4:13

Overtime
God, help me to be calm and courageous during competition. Help me to focus on You, my audience of One.

Ready

Remind the people to be subject to rulers and authorities, to be obedient, to be ready to do whatever is good, to slander no one, to be peaceable and considerate, and to show true humility toward all men.

TITUS 3:1-2, *NIV*

Set

"Whatever." How many times a day do you hear that word? How many times do you say it? We often say it with a shrug or even irritation.

"Whatever . . . I don't really care."
"Whatever . . . I'm tired of thinking about it."
"Whatever . . . Coach will never give me playing time."
"Whatever . . . I quit."

The apostle Paul also used the word "whatever" a lot. His use of "whatever" wasn't about frustration or resignation; it was about completeness and wholehearted commitment. Whatever you are doing (such as studying or practicing), do it for God's glory (see 1 Corinthians 10:31). Whatever gifts you have (such as athletic ability), use them to serve others—be a team player (see Romans 12:6-8). Whatever is excellent or pure or whatever is right, think about those things (see Philippians 4:6-8).

Jesus lived a "whatever" lifestyle. Whatever His Father wanted Him to say or do, He did it. Jesus never questioned His Father's will, because He trusted His Father. And trust is the key to the whatevers.

You can say "whatever" because you don't trust people around you, or you can say "whatever" to Jesus because you trust Him. You can say, "Jesus, I know you want the best for me, so I will say 'whatever' to You and Your will for my life." —*Debbie Haliday*

Go

1. Do you live a "whatever" lifestyle for the Lord?
2. What areas of your life need to move from an apathetic "whatever" to a sold-out "whatever"?
3. What needs to change in your life in order for that to happen?

Workout

Mark 10:35-45; John 11:21; Philippians 4:8-9

Overtime

God, I want my life to be a "whatever" life that brings You honor and glory—both on and off the field. Today I choose to place my trust in You and the plan You have for my life.

Spiritual Muscles

Ready

So then, just as you received Christ Jesus as Lord, continue to live in him, rooted and built up in him, strengthened in the faith as you were taught, and overflowing with thankfulness.

COLOSSIANS 2:6-7, *NIV*

Set

It seems like only yesterday that I was in my high school weight room pumping the weights with the music cranked up to a deafening level. I have no doubt that the thousands of hours I spent in the weight room as a high school, college and professional athlete have paid off throughout my athletic career.

As a young man, I wanted not only to get big but also to excel in my sport. Lifting weights built me up and strengthened me to be the best athlete I could be. The muscle that I added helped me perform better and kept me from injury. Too bad my mom didn't like the fact that my clothes weren't fitting anymore!

In the above passage in Colossians 2:7, Paul writes a powerful truth that as followers of Christ, we need to be "strengthened in the faith." The Lord desires for us to develop spiritual muscles by hitting the spiritual weight room. Our faith grows and has an impact on other lives when we develop spiritual muscles. In 1 Timothy 4:7-8, Paul challenges us to work out and produce spiritual sweat:

> Have nothing to do with godless myths . . . rather, train yourself to be godly. For physical training is of some value, but godliness has value for all things, holding promise for both the present life and the life to come.

You might be wondering what it means to be strong in the Lord. I know that when I am in the weight room, I have a detailed, specific workout routine. Maybe you need the same thing spiritually.

God desires for you to invest the time to develop those spiritual muscles—not for your gain but for His glory! —*Dan Britton*

Go

1. What does it mean to work out spiritually? Can you list some specific ways?
2. When does God desire for you to work out with Him?
3. What is your spiritual routine? What are you doing to be "strengthened in the faith"?

Workout
1 Corinthians 9:25-27; 1 Timothy 4:7-8

Overtime
Lord, I often feel weak spiritually. I know that You desire for me to be strong. Please help me develop the spiritual muscles I need to serve You well. Show me what I should be doing to be strengthened in the faith and let Your strong hands of love guide me.

Ready

Be self-controlled and alert. Your enemy the devil prowls around like a roaring lion looking for someone to devour. Resist him, standing firm in the faith, because you know that your brothers throughout the world are undergoing the same kind of sufferings.

1 PETER 5:8-9, *NIV*

Set

Watch any of the famous *Rocky* movies and you'll find a prime example of someone who never gave up in battle. With every movie, Sylvester Stallone's character, Rocky Balboa, faced an even bigger challenge. Yet through each 12-round beating, he always managed to get back up on his feet and find victory.

The first line of the FCA Competitor's Creed states: "I am a Christian first and last." As Christians we are faced with a battle that rages all around us. Our souls are up for grabs. God has them, but Satan wants them. And if he can't take us with him, he'll make our lives here on Earth the toughest war we'll ever fight. We carry a large target on our backs as believers in Christ. For Satan, there's a higher price on our lives because we work for the Kingdom. The more we grow in Christ and the more people come to know Christ through us, the more Satan loses.

The Competitor's Creed states: "I give my all—all of the time. I do not give up. I do not give in. I do not give out. I am the Lord's warrior—a competitor by conviction and a disciple of determination." A lifetime of war isn't going to be easy. But if we draw on God's grace and God's power, we too can keep getting up round after round. *—Danny Burns*

Go

1. What are the weak links in your armor where Satan attacks you the most?
2. What can you do to strengthen your weak links?

3. Do you draw on God's grace and power each day to fight your spiritual battles?

Workout
Proverbs 4:14-15; Colossians 3:1-5; James 4:7

Overtime
Lord, I know the battle ahead of me isn't going to be easy. Help me to rely on You alone for the strength and wisdom I need. Let me never stop praying for mercy and guidance, and help me to resist temptation. And, Father, please bless me with fellow brothers and sisters who can help me along the way.

Right Place, Right Time

Ready
Who knows but that you have come to royal position for such as time as this?
ESTHER 4:14, *NIV*

Set
The gym was packed with screaming fans. You could cut the tension with a knife. It was late in the fourth quarter and Luke had just come into the game—his first game as a varsity player. With time slowly ticking away, the ball was passed to him. He began to dribble toward the basket and . . . bounced the ball off of his foot and out of bounds. *I am so out of place,* Luke thought. *Why did Coach put me in the game?*

With less than a minute left, Luke's team got the ball back. 10, 9, 8, 7, 6, 5, 4, 3—Luke picked up the ball and was fouled in the process. Now he was going to the line for a bonus one-on-one. Eyeing the basket, he let the first shot go . . . *swish!* Tie game. Luke had risked it all by picking up the loose ball, and now the game was his to win or lose. He took a deep breath and let the ball fly . . . it landed on the side of the rim but then gently slid in. His team had won the game!

In the Old Testament, when King Xerxes was looking for a queen, all the women in the land came to the palace. Esther, of Jewish descent, came as well, and she had the great honor of being chosen as queen. But Esther's uncle Mordecai needed her help—there was a plan to rid the kingdom of all Jews. Esther knew that she had to speak to the king, but in those days to enter the king's presence uninvited was to risk death. So she rallied the people and leaned on the Lord for help. In the end, Esther realized that she was in the right place at the right time for her God and her people.

Sometimes, you may not understand God's plan for your life. But like Esther, when you realize God's purpose for your life, you will feel empowered. Taking a risk is easier when you know God is in control. Esther knew that she could lose her life by going to the king, but that her entire family would die if she did not. She made the right call.

Esther trusted that her God would provide, and He did. Feel out of place in your life? Find God and join Him there. There is always room at the right place and right time with God! —*Jere Johnson*

Go

1. Do you feel out of place at school, on the team or at home?
2. Do you know what God's purpose is for your life?
3. Are you willing to take a risk for God today?

Workout
Esther 8; John 14:15

Overtime
Lord, guide me in Your ways so that I will know how to take a stand for You, just as Esther did. When I start to feel out of place, help me to know You are near. Amen.

Ready

Whatever you do, work at it with all your heart,
as working for the Lord, not for men.

COLOSSIANS 3:23

Set

Last year, I got the chance to play my first college basketball game in my home state. I was so excited to play in front of the 40-plus people who had come to watch. I wanted to play well and prayed that God would help me to do so.

Much to my disappointment, I played the worst game of my life. I made only one shot in my team's humiliating 30-point loss. I was so embarrassed that I didn't want to talk to any of my family or friends who had come to cheer me on. I was afraid of what they thought of me and my performance.

But God taught me something about His love and my worth that night. As I made my way out of the locker room after that game, I was welcomed by smiling faces and warm hugs. The people that had come to see me play didn't care if I had scored three points or 30 points. They just wanted to see the one they loved.

God looks at us in the same way. First John 3:1 states, "Look at how great a love the Father has given us, that we should be called God's children. And we are! The reason the world does not know us is that it didn't know Him." God loves us enough to call us His children. He sees our hearts and does not base His love on our actions or performance. We are loved unconditionally by our Maker. All God wants is for us to do the best we can with the gifts that He's given us.

As athletes, we have a choice: to find our worth in our performance on the athletic field or to find our worth in something more lasting. Sports just happen to be the things that we do, but they do not define who we are or how much we're worth. As a Christian, above anything else, you are a loved and valued child of God.

—*Jess Hansen*

Go

1. What defines you?
2. For whom were you honestly competing in your last performance?
3. Do you believe that you are unconditionally loved by God?

Workout

Psalm 108:1; 2 Corinthians 2:14-15; Ephesians 1:3-6; 1 John 3:1

Overtime

Lord, thank You for calling me Your child. Help me to live in such a way as to reflect Your perfect love.

The Gap

Ready

I know, my God, that You test the heart and that You are pleased with uprightness. I have willingly given all these things with an upright heart, and now I have seen Your people who are present here giving joyfully and willingly to You.

1 CHRONICLES 29:17

Set

The Competitor's Creed states: "My attitude on and off the field is above reproach—my conduct beyond criticism." This is a tough standard. Legendary Hall of Fame basketball coach John Wooden once said:

A leader's most powerful ally is his or her own example. There is hypocrisy to the phrase "Do as I say, not as I do." I refused to make demands on my boys that I wasn't willing to live out in my own life.

As athletes and coaches, we too often desire to live a life that we know we have not committed in our hearts to living. We desire for our external life (the life that everyone sees—our wins and accomplishments) to be greater than our internal life (the life that no one sees—our thoughts and desires).

The best definition of hypocrisy that I have ever heard is that it is the gap that exists between the public life and the private life. It's the difference between the external life and the internal life. God doesn't want there to be a gap at all. He wants every aspect of our lives to be filled with integrity.

As competitors, there is a constant war in our souls. We do not want others to see us as we really are. We are afraid that the gap will be exposed. However, God desires the exact opposite. He wants us to bring the dark things that we have buried in our hearts into the light so that He can purify us.

Oswald Chambers wrote, "My worth to God in public is what I am in private."[17] As a competitor for Christ, be committed to being real—gap free! —*Dan Britton*

Go

1. Where are the gaps in your life?
2. As a competitor, do you expect something from your teammates or peers that you are not willing to commit to yourself?
3. What does it mean to be a "real" competitor?

Workout
Psalms 25:21; 78:72; Proverbs 10:9; Titus 2:6-8

Overtime
Lord, I pray that You will reveal to me any gaps in my life.
I desire to live and play for You as an authentic competitor.
It is by Your strength and power that those gaps can be closed.
Thank You for making me complete by Your grace.

Fire in My Belly

Ready

The words are fire in my belly, a burning in my bones. I'm worn out trying to hold it in. I can't do it any longer!

JEREMIAH 20:9, *THE MESSAGE*

Set

"Do you have fire in your belly?" is a question I've heard hundreds of times from coaches. It was never really a question that I was supposed to answer; rather, it was a challenge to play harder and tougher. Basically, coaches wanted to know if I had the passion and determination to play with a competitive edge.

As an athlete, I never had the natural ability of others (speed, strength, size), but I did have the fire in my belly. For me, the fire was hustle, grit and tenacity to get the job done—whatever Coach asked of me! I was the player who always gave 100 percent, right up until the whistle blew. My goal was to leave it all on the field during practice and during games.

Sometimes I wonder if I have the fire in my belly when it comes to my spiritual life. Jeremiah says that he had a fire burning so strong for God that he couldn't contain it. The spiritual hustle, the spiritual grit, and the spiritual tenacity all need to burn within us so fiercely that we can't hold them back. Can you imagine finally confessing to a teammate, "I'm tired of withholding Jesus from you. It's burning so strongly inside of me that I have no choice but to share Jesus with you." That would be incredible!

The passion for our Lord should be like a fire that rages within. However, we must also remember that the fire comes from Him. We must lay ourselves on the altar and ask God to consume us with His fire. The great preacher John Wesley said that large crowds came to hear him preach during the Great Awakening because "I set myself on fire and people come to watch me burn." Are you on fire for Jesus?

—*Dan Britton*

1. What do you think of when you hear the phrase "a spiritual fire in the belly"?
2. What does it mean to have spiritual grit and tenacity?
3. What would happen if you confessed to your teammates that you are tired of withholding Jesus from them?

Workout
Psalm 84:1-2

Overtime
Lord, I have competitive fire in my belly, but I also want that spiritual fire. Consume me with Your fire, Jesus. Let the fire that burns within be a light in the darkness that surrounds me.

Six Percent

Ready
They will turn away from hearing the truth and will turn aside to myths. But as for you, keep a clear head about everything, endure hardship, do the work of an evangelist, fulfill your ministry.

2 TIMOTHY 4:4-5

Set
A recent study reports that only 6 percent of teens today believe that moral truth is absolute. I knew it wouldn't be high, but that's really low. Not good. Young people today are basically saying that life is a sliding scale. Truth has become relative because it all depends on the situation.

In the world of athletics, there are many truths that cannot be relative, such as wins and losses. Imagine if every athlete defined winning differently—one by score, one by hustle, one by the best fans, and so on. It would be chaos! Fortunately—or unfortunately—winning is defined by the scoreboard. Life without truths, absolutes and boundaries leads to chaos.

Psalm 31:5 states that the Lord is the God of truth. God is our standard, and His Word isn't just filled with truth, it *is* the truth. Many of us embrace the absolute truth (Jesus Christ), but we find it hard to apply that truth to others. We feel as if we are judging or condemning. It's a hard line to walk, but remember that absolute truth is for everyone. And God wants to use us in the lives of others to help them understand that His truth can set them free.

We must hold fast to the truth and not compromise under any circumstances. As it states in Proverbs 23:23, "Buy the truth and do not sell it; get wisdom, discipline and understanding" (*NIV*). We need to stand for the truth on and off the field of competition. We must not sell out.

So, are you part of the "Six Percent" Club or the "Ninety-Four Percent" Club? —*Dan Britton*

Go

1. How do you define truth? How would your friends define it?
2. When do you find it the most difficult to stand for the truth?
3. What happens when you do stand for the truth? Do others respect you, or do you experience ridicule, name-calling and isolation?

Workout
John 18:8; Romans 1:25; Ephesians 1:13

Overtime
Lord, I know You are the Truth. Help me to have a clear head and pure heart so that truth is not compromised. Thank You for filling me with Your Holy Spirit so that the absolute truth is manifested. I desire to be Your agent of transformation by living and playing by Your truth. Amen.

Ready

I also consider everything to be a loss in view of the surpassing value of knowing Christ Jesus my Lord.

PHILIPPIANS 3:8

Set

As the Competitor's Creed states, your desire as an athlete is to "compete for the pleasure of [your] Heavenly Father, the honor of Christ and the reputation of the Holy Spirit." That is truly competing with a spiritual focus, not a physical focus.

On July 25, 2003, Andrii Serdinov, a Ukrainian swimmer, experienced five brief minutes of glory when he achieved his lifelong goal of setting a world record in the 100-meter butterfly. He was pumped—celebrating and throwing his hands in the air! His joy, however, was short-lived, and his time in the spotlight disappeared just as quickly as it had arrived. Five minutes later, 18-year-old U.S. swimmer Michael Phelps broke Serdinov's world record. It happened so fast that Serdinov could not even finish one interview about his incredible accomplishment.

Fame is like the wealth described in Proverbs 23:5: "Cast but a glance at riches, and they are gone, for they will surely sprout wings and fly off to the sky like an eagle" (NIV). Often, as soon as fame is achieved, it is gone. The glory that is of this world will never last. As athletes, we strive to be the best, but we cannot hold on to our accomplishments. We must offer them to the Lord to be used for His glory.

The glory that the world offers is rubbish. It will all be destroyed. The only thing that will last is God's kingdom. Too many athletes would rather have five minutes of worldly fame than any amount of eternal glory. As an athlete, seek first the kingdom of God, and if He blesses you with five minutes of glory, make sure that you offer it back to Him. Don't keep it for yourself. You have been created in the likeness of God Almighty so that you might bring Him glory! —Dan Britton

Go

1. What are some of the awards you have received?
2. Have you ever given God the credit for an achievement?
3. Why is it so hard to focus on the eternal things and so easy to focus on the things that are temporary?

Workout

John 12:25; 2 Corinthians 4:16-18

Overtime

Lord, please forgive me for getting awards and records for my own gain. I do not want to be a selfish athlete. I want to be a surrendered athlete. I pray that I will compete to bring You glory.

In One Ear

Ready

Do not merely listen to the word, and so deceive yourselves. Do what it says.
JAMES 1:22, *NIV*

Set

I read a newspaper article last year about a professional baseball player who couldn't seem to make the necessary adjustments needed in his approach to hitting. The player contended that his hitting was fine, but many of his current and former coaches disagreed. They pointed to the fact that his batting average had continued to decline and that he was striking out at an alarming rate.

In one game, the player might have 3 hits, but in the next 4 games he wouldn't get a hit, striking out 9 times. It's not that the player didn't have good coaching—one of his previous coaches was a former batting champion. The problem was that he wasn't doing what the coaches were asking. James 1:22-24 says:

Be doers of the word, and not hearers only, deceiving yourselves. For if anyone is a hearer of the word and not a doer, he is like a man observing his natural face in a mirror; for he observes himself, goes away, and immediately forgets what kind of man he was (*NKJV*).

A man who listens but does not put what he has heard into action immediately forgets what kind of man he is.

The recipe for consistent success is found in James 1:25: "But he who looks into the perfect law of liberty and continues in it, and is not a forgetful hearer but a doer of the work, this one will be blessed in what he does" (*NKJV*). Clearly, we see that if we listen to God and our coaches and do what they say, we will be blessed in what we do.

It is not enough to simply hear about something, know about it or even talk about it; you must live it. Just because you listen to God and your coaches, it doesn't mean that you will do what they ask. You must do it! —*Marc Agnello*

Go

1. Are you a listener but not a doer?
2. In what areas of your life do you need to put into action what you have heard?
3. As a competitor, what in your life makes it difficult for you to put your coach's advice into practice? How can you overcome that difficulty?

Workout

Galatians 6:19; Ephesians 6:6; 2 Thessalonians 3:11,13; Hebrews 13:16

Overtime

Lord, please help me live out Your Word in my daily life.
I fall short so often, but I trust that with Your help,
I can be a living witness to the gospel. Amen.

Ready

When Haman saw that Mordecai would not kneel down or pay him honor, he was enraged. Yet having learned who Mordecai's people were, he scorned the idea of killing only Mordecai. Instead Haman looked for a way to destroy all Mordecai's people, the Jews.

ESTHER 3:5, *NIV*

Ready

Hannah made the varsity tennis team as a sophomore and eventually beat out Mindy, a senior, for the number 2 singles spot. Hannah soon became very arrogant in her new position of power on the team. She began to boss her teammates around and tell them to do things for her. But Mindy did not budge. This made Hannah very angry, and she soon began to do anything to make Mindy look bad at practice in front of the coaches. Mindy did not retaliate; she went about her business playing doubles in her final year. Hannah would not let up. Her dislike for Mindy turned into hatred, and she tried to get Mindy kicked off the team. Does this sound familiar?

Back in Esther's day, a man named Haman rose in power until he became second in command behind Xerxes. He was ruthless and arrogant. He demanded respect and enforced his power over the people. But Mordecai, Esther's cousin, was not about to give in to him. Haman was severely hateful to Mordecai and the entire Jewish race and wanted to kill them all. But Haman thought too much of himself, and he soon became his own worst enemy. He died on the very gallows that he had built to hang Mordecai.

Hannah's plan to get rid of Mindy also backfired, and she was kicked off the team because of her attitude and hatred toward Mindy. Mindy went on to regain her position and began to win for her team. Hannah, like Haman, got just what she deserved. Power and self-importance are the downfall of many. Mindy, like Mordecai, held her ground, had self-respect and followed a better way. —*Jere Johnson*

Go

1. How much of Hannah or Haman is inside of you?
2. Do you desire to control others or let them control you?
3. Do you want to take revenge when your pride has been wounded?

Workout

2 Chronicles 26

Overtime

*Lord, I confess that I often want to be in total control.
Sometimes I even want to control others. Forgive me for
trying to control people and situations, because I know that
You are the only one that is in total control.*

Workout Partners

Ready

For I want very much to see you, that I may
impart to you some spiritual gift to strengthen you,
that is, to be mutually encouraged by each
other's faith, both yours and mine.

ROMANS 1:11-12

Set

A workout partner is someone who will be there for you. It is a person who has your same desire to succeed and who can't wait to train with you. It is someone who can't wait to be energized by your energy level.

In Paul's letter to the church in Rome, it is apparent that he couldn't wait to see the believers there and spend time with them. He was excited to help them train. He was excited to tell them about Jesus. He was excited to work with them and to be mutually encouraged by them.

We all need a workout partner who will help us in our spiritual training. We need someone who will make sure that we are reading our Bible each day. We need a partner who will commit to growing his or her own relationship with Jesus right alongside of us. We need someone who will give us the support we need when we are going through the rough stretches.

We all need someone who can encourage us and whom we can encourage. —*Michael Hill*

Go

1. Who is your athletic workout partner? Who is your spiritual workout partner? What similarities do you see in the ways that each of you train?
2. How does your partner's attitude affect yours? What does that say about how your attitude affects him or her?
3. How can you take your spiritual workouts up a notch?

Workout

Proverbs 27:17; Ecclesiastes 4:11-12; Hebrews 3:13; 10:25; 1 John 1:3-4

Overtime

Father, let me find encouragement today from my Christian brothers and sisters. Let me be an encouragement to them also. Use me to build Your church. Bring me together with people who will help grow my relationship with You. Provide me with people who can be an encouragement to me, and let me be an encouragement to them in return. I thank You for fellowship, Father. In Jesus' name, amen.

"Two are better than one because they have a good reward for their efforts.

For if either falls, his companion can lift him up; but pity the one who falls without another to lift him up" (Ecclesiastes 4:9-10).

Give Me Credit

Ready

The purpose is that none of you will be inflated with pride in favor of one person over another. For who makes you so superior? What do you have that you didn't receive? If, in fact, you did receive it, why do you boast as if you hadn't received it? Already you are full! Already You are rich! You have begun to reign as kings without us.

1 CORINTHIANS 4:6-8

Set

Everybody wants to get the glory. Why shouldn't we? It feels good to have someone say that we played a good game. It feels good when someone compliments us on our athleticism. It feels good to hear our name over the loud speaker after a good play. The problem is that we haven't done anything to deserve this glory.

Paul told the church at Corinth that everything they possessed came to them because they had received it. This means that they didn't have anything at all that God had not given to them. Most of our society today has forgotten this lesson.

How many times does a football player score a touchdown and do a celebratory dance that draws attention to himself? How many times does a basketball player make a shot and then draw attention to himself or herself? How many times during the summer does a baseball or softball player pause to watch a home run soar over the outfield fence?

All of this draws attention to people who don't deserve the glory. God provided everything we have. He gave us birth. He gives us our talents. If He gives us the talent to score a touchdown, a three-point shot or a home run, why do we not give Him the credit for allowing us to receive that talent? —*Michael Hill*

Go

1. Who received the glory the last time someone complimented you on a good game?

2. Who gave you the talents that you have?
3. How many times do you give God the credit for blessing you with your talents?

Workout
1 Corinthians 1:30-31; 2 Corinthians 9:10-11; James 1:16-18

Overtime
Father, thank You for giving me life. Thank You for giving me the ability to glorify You on the athletic field. Thank You for using me to build Your kingdom. Today, I pray that my performance will glorify You and You alone. I don't want to accept any of the credit for what You will do today, Father. Help me to continually point others to You. In the name of Christ, I pray. Amen.

Smack

Ready
Jesus answered, "I am the way and the truth and the life. No one comes to the Father except through me."
JOHN 14:6, *NIV*

Set
We hear it on ESPN, read it in the papers and see it on the nightly news—"smack." What is it? Well, smack is the common form of vernacular jargon that some players and coaches use to dramatize or publicize their performances or future endeavors. In short, it is trash-talking.

In every league, game and team, you will find someone who has the gift of talking smack. Usually, the person who talks this way has an ego the size of Texas but humility the size of Delaware and common sense the size of an M&M. Smack talkers can talk the talk, but they rarely walk the walk.

Back in Jerusalem, there was a group of men who could talk spiritual smack with the best of them. We know them as the Pharisees—

and Caiaphas was the top dog of his day. But the funny thing was that Caiaphas and his buddies thought Jesus and His followers were the trash talkers. But Jesus only spoke the truth.

No verse better illustrates this than John 14:6, where Jesus said that the only way into heaven is through Him. Many thought that such a claim was truly smack of the greatest kind. Some even called it blasphemy. Surely this man could not back up what He was saying!

But they found out very quickly that Jesus could both talk the talk and walk the walk. Jesus *is* the only way, the only truth and the only life, and *no one* will get to the Father if they don't go through Him.

So let me encourage you to not talk smack. Let your walk— your godly walk—do the talking for you. Live your life for Christ because He has given you the way, the truth and the life that leads back to Him. Jesus did all the talking for us. We just need to fol- low His example. Make sure your walk matches your spiritual talk!
—*Jere Johnson*

Go

1. Are you a smack talker, athletically or spiritually speaking?
2. Does your walk match your talk?
3. What do you need to change to be more like Christ?

Workout
John 11:24-27; Ephesians 4:17-32; 1 Timothy 4:6-9

Overtime
Lord, help me guard my tongue. Develop in me a godly character that speaks for itself. Show me where I need to allow the Holy Sprit to cleanse me so that I can be more like Christ. I give you all the glory. Amen.

Ready

You have heard that it was said, An eye for an eye and a tooth for a tooth. But I tell you, don't resist an evildoer. On the contrary, if anyone slaps you on your right cheek, turn the other to him also.

MATTHEW 5:38-39

Set

When the 2004 NBA Western Conference semifinal series between the Minnesota Timberwolves and the Sacramento Kings began heating up, tempers started flaring. Kings guard Anthony Peeler hit former teammate Kevin Garnett in the face with an elbow during the third quarter of Game 6 and was immediately ejected from the game. "It was retaliation after [Garnett] hit me with an elbow," said Peeler.[18]

Retaliation is a natural response when we feel we have been wronged. If others hurt us, we want to hurt them back so that they know how it feels. We want them to feel the pain we feel. However, as Christians our desire is to live as Jesus did, so we must look at how He handled injustice. The Bible addresses this in several places, one of which is 1 Peter 2:21,23:

> For you were called to this, because Christ also suffered for you, leaving you an example, so that you should follow in His steps . . . when reviled, He did not revile in return; when suffering, He did not threaten, but committed Himself to the One who judges justly.

As a Christian competitor, know that handling inappropriate behavior aimed at you doesn't mean you can't play hard. We should play hard—not to pay back another person, but to honor the Lord and help our team win. —*Josh Carter*

Go

1. Have you experienced personal attacks in competition?

2. Why is it important to handle these personal assaults the way that Jesus did?

3. What do you find in 1 Peter 3:12-14 that could help you?

Workout

Proverbs 20:22; Romans 12:19-21; 1 Thessalonians 5:15;
1 Peter 2:19-21

Overtime

*Father, help me compete in a way that reveals
Jesus' presence in me. Help me turn the other cheek,
even when I don't feel like it.*

Hooked Up

Ready

Suddenly a sound like the blowing of a violent wind came from heaven and filled the whole house where they were sitting. They saw what seemed to be tongues of fire that separated and came to rest on each of them.

ACTS 2:2-3, *NIV*

Set

As athletes, we train to become faster and stronger. We try to bring as much power to our sport as we can. We may engage in a weight-training program. We may go out and run. We may attend a sports camp. But even more important than our physical training is our spiritual training.

Consider a plain, ordinary lightbulb. How much power does it put out? On its own, it puts out absolutely none. It has to be hooked to a power source in order to produce light.

This reminds me of the apostle Peter, a very interesting person. He was a common man (a fisherman by trade) but also a powerful man. And we certainly have to agree that Peter was dedicated to his calling.

Peter said he would never be drawn away from the Lord (see Matthew 26:33-35). But what happened after Jesus was arrested? Peter denied Jesus—not once but three times (see Matthew 26:74-75). However, later on, at Pentecost, Peter boldly proclaimed the gospel and was instrumental in bringing thousands to the Lord (see Acts 2:14-41).

What made the difference? The time spent waiting on the Lord and the indwelling of the Holy Spirit. Isaiah 40:31 states:

> Those who hope in the Lord
> will renew their strength.
> They will soar on wings like eagles;
> they will run and not grow weary,
> they will walk and not be faint (*NIV*).

Today, make sure you're connected to the Power Source. —*Ken Bakewell*

Go

1. How did Peter stumble?
2. What happens when you wait on the Lord? How can you be hooked up to the Power Source?
3. What has God promised to do if you accept Christ and rely on Him as your source of power?

Workout
Isaiah 40:31; Matthew 26:31-75; Philippians 4:13,19

Overtime
*Lord, You are my power source. Please forgive me for
the times that I have tried to replace You with some other source.
You are my strength. I will wait upon You. Fill me with
Your Spirit of power and might. Anoint me with boldness
to proclaim Your message. Amen.*

Blessed is a man who endures trials,
because when he passes the test he will
receive the crown of life that He has promised
to those who love Him.

JAMES 1:12

Set

God doesn't always work the way we think He should. Sometimes the things that we think are tragedies turn out to be blessings. In the Bible, Joseph serves as the perfect example of tragedy-turned-blessing. When Joseph received a dream foreshadowing his role to reign over his brothers, his brothers grew angry and sold him into slavery. When Joseph was later falsely accused of a crime and thrown into prison, it seemed that his dream would never come true.

But the Lord proved faithful and present. "The Lord was with Joseph and extended kindness to him" (Genesis 39:21). While in prison, Joseph attracted attention with his God-given ability to interpret dreams. He was soon given the opportunity to interpret Pharaoh's dream. Through that interpretation, he was able to give Pharaoh the advice he needed to save his people from years of famine. As a result, Pharaoh put Joseph in charge of the whole land of Egypt. Joseph went from being a slave to being the ruler of Egypt. Talk about a tragedy being turned into a blessing! And it wasn't just Joseph who was blessed—all of Egypt was spared from a famine in the process.

Often, God takes everything away to show that He has so much more in store for us if we will only have patience and faith. After we have endured a trial, it's easy to look back and see how God was working in and through us. But it is when we are in the middle of it— day by day—that it seems interminable and hopeless. That is where patience and faith come in. We must believe that God is still with us as He promises and that He will bring us through into something better—His ultimate blessing. —*Loren Thornburg*

Go

1. Can you remember an event that seemed like a tragedy but turned out to be a blessing?
2. Can you see how God was working in this event?
3. How will you apply this to your life?

Workout

Genesis 45:4-7; Romans 5:1-5; Hebrews 10:19-25; James 1:2-6

Overtime

God, You promise that if I delight myself in You, You will give me the desires of my heart. I choose to stand on these promises in faith and wait expectantly for what You are going to do in my life.

The Ultimate Pregame Meal

Ready

"My food is to do the will of Him who sent Me and to finish His work," Jesus told them. "Don't you say, 'There are still four more months, then comes the harvest'? Listen to what I'm telling you: Open your eyes and look at the fields, for they are ready for harvest."

JOHN 4:34-35

Set

As athletes, what we put into our bodies is very important. The pregame meal, in particular, may be the most important meal we eat. We have to make sure we get enough energy to last through the entire competition. This is our last chance to get the fuel we need.

In John 4:34, Jesus tells us of work that will actually *give* us energy instead of using it. Doing God's work will give us the fuel we need in order to succeed in the game of life. So what is the work that we should be doing? In Matthew 28:19-20, Jesus tells us very plainly what our work should be:

Go, therefore, and make disciples of all nations, baptizing them in the name of the Father and of the Son and of the Holy Spirit, teaching them to observe everything I have commanded you.

We are to go out among the nations to build the kingdom of God. As part of Team Jesus Christ, I challenge you to devote yourself to this kind of work.

The mission of FCA is to "Present to coaches and athletes and all whom they influence the challenge and adventure of receiving Jesus Christ as Savior and Lord and serving Him in their relationships and in the fellowship of the church." Pay attention to how doing this feeds your soul. Make note of the energy it gives you. You may never look at food the same way again. —*Michael Hill*

Go

1. Are you seeking to do God's work daily? Are you asking God to show you where He wants you to work?
2. Are you studying God's Word each day to become a better worker?
3. What can you do today to feed your soul so that you will have the fuel you need to succeed in the game of life?

Workout
Psalm 119:164; Matthew 6:11; 28:18-20; Acts 1:8; 17:11

Overtime
Lord, show me where You want me to work, and I will serve You. Put the people in front of me whom You want me to talk to today. Let Your words be heard with my voice. Take this life and use it to build Your kingdom. In the name of Jesus Christ, I pray, amen.

Ready

But you will receive power when the Holy Spirit comes on you; and you will be my witnesses in Jerusalem, and in all Judea and Samaria, and to the ends of the earth.

ACTS 1:8, *NIV*

Set

There had not been an undefeated Kentucky Derby winner since Seattle Slew did it in 1977. Fans watching the 2004 Kentucky Derby saw a Pennsylvania-bred horse named Smarty Jones, with a trainer and a jockey who were both rookies, end the 27-year drought by winning the race, running the horse's record to 7–0. Jockey Stewart Elliott later said:

> It is just unbelievable. We bunched up a bit on the first turn but things turned out great. It was a good trip. I crossed the wire and I can't explain it; there aren't words to describe it. At the three-eighths pole, I knew I had a loaded gun underneath me. I was just going to sit until he straightened up and switched leads. He really went to running.[19]

Stewart Elliott knew it wasn't his power that was going to win the Kentucky Derby but that it was the power of his horse that would carry him across the finish line. In the same way, it is the power of the Holy Spirit that is carrying us to the finish line in the race of life.

Through His power, the Holy Spirit also sets us free from the law of sin and death, speaks God's words through us, convicts our hearts of sin, strengthens us in our weakness and enables us to live the life of obedience that God desires for us. —*Josh Carter*

Go

1. When do you feel most powerful in athletics?
2. How have you seen the power of the Holy Spirit at work in your life?

3. In what part of your life do you most need the power of the Holy Spirit right now?

Workout
1 Samuel 16:13; Romans 15:13; 1 Corinthians 2:4-5

Overtime
Lord, thank You for the power of the Holy Spirit and for the amazing ways it moves in my life. Continue to speak to me, Lord. Instruct me and show me how I can grow in my relationship with You. I love You and I praise You, amen.

For the Glory

Ready
No wise man, enchanter, magician or diviner can explain to the king the mystery he has asked about, but there is a God in heaven who reveals mysteries. He has shown King Nebuchadnezzar what will happen in days to come.

DANIEL 2:27-28, *NIV*

Set
As competitors, it is often difficult for us to give glory where glory is due. Training, discipline, perseverance and drive are all characteristics that can propel us to the next level, as we go from being good athletes to being great ones. Often after achieving a goal, we feel that it is our hard work that got us to that point. The praise, honor and glory are focused on us as individual athletes.

Daniel had the chance to take the glory for himself, but instead he chose to give it to the Lord. "No wise man, enchanter, magician or diviner can explain to the king the mystery he has asked about, but there is a God in heaven who reveals mysteries," he told the King

(Daniel 2:27). "The great God has shown the king what will take place in the future. The dream is true and the interpretation is trustworthy" (Daniel 2:45).

The FCA Competitor's Creed states:

> I do not trust in myself.
> I do not boast in my abilities or believe in my own strength.
> I rely solely on the power of God.
> I compete for the pleasure of my Heavenly Father, the honor of Christ and the reputation of the Holy Spirit.

The results of our efforts must result in God's glory. To accept glory for ourselves is to rob God of His glory. *—Dan Britton*

Go

1. As an athlete, how much confidence do you have in your own abilities? Do you trust only in yourself?
2. What does it mean to compete for the joy of the heavenly Father?
3. If Daniel had scored the winning goal or been awarded the team's MVP award, what would have been his response?

Workout
2 Corinthians 5:1-10

Overtime
Lord, it is difficult for me to give You all the glory.
Please forgive me for often taking the credit when, in reality, my athletic accomplishments should be a fragrant offering to You.
In my next competition, help me to understand that the results of my efforts must result in Your glory.

1. "Gordon Rallies to Win Third Daytona 500," NASCAR, February 21, 2005. http://www.nascar.com/2005/news/headlines/cup/02/20/bc.car.nascar. daytona50.ap/ (accessed October 2005).

2. "Under Armour Shirts," Goldman Bros., October 12, 2005. http://www. goldmanbros.com/under-armour/under-armour-shirts.php (accessed October 2005).

3. Vince Lombardi, quoted in "NFL Legends: Vince Lombardi," About.com. http://football.about.com/cs/legends/p/vincelombardi.htm (accessed October 2005).

4. Jake Delhomme, quoted in "Motivation According to Delhomme," Talking About ProFootball.com. http://www.talkaboutprofootball.com/group /alt.sports.football.pro.ne-patriots/messages/303135.html (accessed October 2005).

5. *Webster's Dictionary,* 11th edition, s.v. "strife."

6. Freddy Adu, quoted in "Freddy Adu First Pick in MLS Draft," *Red Nova News.* http://www.rednova.com/news/general/40116/freddy_adu_first_pick_in_ mls_draft/ (accessed October 2005).

7. Star Parker, "Role Models Matter," *WorldNetDaily.* http://www.worldnet daily.com/news/article.asp?ARTICLE_ID=36201 (accessed October 4, 2005).

8. "University Denies Sex Party Allegations," CNN Law Center, January 31, 2004. http://www.cnn.com/2004/LAW/01/31/university.assault.case.reut/ (accessed October 2005).

9. Les Carpenter, "Diary of a Downfall: The Neuheisel Story," *The Dallas Morning News.* http://apse.dallasnews.com/contest/2003/writing/100- 250/100-250.explanatory.third.html (accessed October 2005).

10. Pete Carroll, quoted in Kelly Whiteside, "USC's Carroll Speaks Highly of Top Ranking," *USA Today* online version. http://www.usatoday.com/sports/ college/football/pac10/2005-01-06-carroll-usc-future_x.htm (accessed October 2005.

11. Norm Eash, quoted in "Illinois Wesleyan Mourns Death of Football Co-Captain," Illinois Wesleyen University. http://www2.iwu.edu/newsre lease05/std_schmied.shtml (accessed October 4, 2005).

12. Jason White, quoted in "White Beats Out Fitzgerald for Heisman Trophy," *SI.com,* Dec. 13, 2003. http://sportsillustrated.cnn.com/2003/football/ncaa/12/13/white.heisman.ap/ (accessed October 2005).

13. "NFL Wants to Halt Celebration Stunts," MSNBC, December 19, 2003. http://msnbc.msn.com/id/3753387/ (accessed October 2005).

14. Michael Campbell, quoted in "Answering the Call," *GolfDigest.com.* http://www.golfdigest.com/majors/usopen/index.ssf?/majors/usopen/2005usopen.html (accessed October 2005).

15. Ibid.

16. *Webster's Dictionary,* 11th edition, s.v. "focus."

17. Oswald Chambers, *My Utmost for His Highest* (Grand Rapids, MI: Discovery House Publishers, 1992), March 17th reading.

18. Anthony Peeler, quoted in Oscar Dixon, "Kings Lose Peeler for Game 7," *USA Today* online version. http://www.usatoday.com/sports/basketball/nba/kings/2004-05-17-peeler-suspension_x.htm (accessed October 2005).

19. Stewart Elliott, quoted in "2004 Kentucky Derby Results," Horse-Races.Net. http://www.horse-races.net/library/derby04-results.htm (accessed October 6, 2005).

Marc Agnello is one of the Huddle coaches of the Wellsville High School FCA Huddle in Wellsville, New York.

Ken Bakewell is a retired teacher and wrestling coach and now serves as the senior instructor at Kids Karate of Warren, an evangelistic Christian outreach in Pennsylvania.

Jay Beard is athletic director, teacher and coach of boys' varsity soccer and basketball at Frederick Christian Academy in Frederick, Maryland. Before coming to Frederick Christian Academy, Jay taught and coached soccer, basketball and softball in Miami, Florida.

Dr. Julie Bell was a gymnast, diver and college cheerleader. As a sports psychologist, Dr. Bell helps coaches, athletes and teams compete at their highest level by working on the mental side of performance.

Dan Britton serves as the Senior Vice President of Ministries of FCA at the national headquarters in Kansas City, Missouri. In high school and college, Dan was a standout lacrosse player. Dan and family reside in Overland Park, Kansas.

Danny Burns is Manager of Online Ministry at FCA's national headquarters in Kansas City, Missouri. Danny served as a huddle leader and varsity distance runner at Northwest Missouri State University and has a passion for advancing the college ministry at FCA.

Josh Carter is the Area Director for North Central Illinois FCA. He is a former high school coach and teacher.

Fleceia Comeaux serves as the area director for the South Houston FCA office. She is a graduate of the University of Houston, where she played basketball and soccer for the Coogs.

Amanda Cromwell played soccer at the collegiate and professional levels and was part of the American '96 Women's Olympic Soccer Team (which won a Gold Medal) and the '95 World Cup Team (which won a Bronze Medal). Amanda is currently the head coach at the University of Central Florida in Orlando, Florida.

Jean Driscoll won two Olympic silver medals and 12 paralympic medals during her career as an elite wheelchair racer. Jean has won numerous prestigious awards and was recognized by *Sports Illustrated for Women* as one of the top 25 female athletes of the twentieth century.

Jill Ewert is a central Kansas native and the editor of FCA's *Sharing the Victory* magazine. Jill is a graduate of the University of Kansas and holds a degree in Sport Science.

Steve Fitzhugh is the founder and executive director of PowerMoves, a national youth organization that uses the power of athletics, academics and the arts to help youth move into success and significance. Steve is also a national spokesperson for FCA's "One Way 2 Play—Drug Free!" program.

Harry Flaherty played professional football for the Philadelphia Eagles, Tampa Bay Bandits, Baltimore Stars and the Dallas Cowboys. Harry currently serves as the New Jersey FCA Director.

Dan Frost is one of the best basketball players to come out of the University of Iowa. Dan played in the NBA for the Milwaukee Bucks and now works with political leaders in Washington, D.C., where he hosts weekly Bible studies on Capitol Hill.

Charles Gee is an FCA staff member serving the Midlands, South Carolina, area. Charles is a former high school teacher and coach.

Debbie Haliday coaches middle school and high school girls' basketball at Hillcrest Christian School in Granada Hills, California. She attended UCLA where she was a member of both the women's softball and basketball teams, receiving honors as an all-regional second baseman and as an all-conference guard. She is also Regional Camp Director for Southern California FCA. Debbie and her family live in Southern California.

Jess Hansen was a standout basketball player at the University of Santa Barbara, California, and one of the greatest three-point threats in UCSB history. After graduation, Jess played professional basketball in Germany.

Alex Harb is a student-athlete.

Michael Hill has served as a football coach at both the college and high school levels. He is now the FCA Area Representative for Southeast Kansas and lives with his family in Winfield, Kansas.

Brad Holloway is an FCA Huddle Coach. Brad teaches and coaches football and wrestling at Union Grove Middle School in McDonough, Georgia.

Elliot Johnson has been a collegiate head coach for 25 years—7 of which he has spent at Olivet Nazarene University, where he is currently the head baseball coach. Coach Johnson's teams have won 11 conference, district or national titles and have appeared in 2 NAIA World Series.

Jere Johnson is a former basketball coach for Indiana Wesleyan University, Oklahoma Wesleyan University and Lakeview Christian School. He currently serves as an FCA staff member in the greater Chicago area.

Carl Miller played with the Dallas Cowboys for the legendary Coach Tom Landry. Carl speaks to many groups and is on staff with FCA in the Greater Fort Worth, Texas, area. He loves working with athletes of all ages and continues to encourage other professional athletes in their faith.

Kerry O'Neill is originally from Iowa and played basketball for Oral Roberts University in Tulsa, Oklahoma, and in 11 different countries. Kerry and his family make their home in Fredericksburg, Virginia, where Kerry serves as FCA Director.

Joe Outlaw is a former collegiate football player and is currently a volunteer community baseball and football coach in the Atlanta area. Joe is the director of Human Resources with the North American Mission Board and also serves on the Board of Directors for the Metro Atlanta FCA.

Jimmy Page serves as both the executive director of the FCA Fitness Ministry and as the general manager of the Maryland Athletic Club. Jimmy and his family live outside of Baltimore, Maryland.

Heather Price attends Toccoa Falls College in Toccoa, Georgia. She was cocaptain of FCA at Winder-Barrow High School, where she played soccer for four years. She currently plays on the intramural kickball team and is involved in FCA at Toccoa Falls.

John Register is a paralympian silver medalist. John speaks at FCA Camps and Huddles.

Roxanne Robbins is the announcer and producer of Faith Beyond the Game, a nationally-syndicated radio program that airs weekly on SRN News. Roxanne was an official chaplain for athletes competing in the 1998 Winter Olympics in Nagano, Japan, and is a regular contributor to *Sports Spectrum* magazine.

Kyle Shultz is a graduate of Greenville College in Illinois, where he received a degree in Student Ministry and played basketball for the Panthers. Kyle and his wife live in Springfield, Illinois.

Judy Siegle is a two-time paralympian and U.S. national record holder in track events for quadriplegic women. Judy is also an author and just published her first book, *Living Without Limits: Ten Keys to Unlocking the Champion in You.*

Kande Speers is a graduate of West Chester University and a two-time lacrosse All-American. Kande currently serves as one of the area's top youth coaches and has also helped coach the FCA Women's Elite College Team.

Loren Thornburg was a pitcher for four years on the University of California Santa Barbara softball team. Loren is currently a graduate assistant softball coach at Augusta State University in Georgia.

Stan Smith is a member of the Board of Directors of Northern Virginia FCA. Stan is a triathlete and works with NovaFCA's Tri4Christ outreach, a sports-specific ministry directed at triathletes. Stan lives in Vienna, Virginia, with his family.

Thanks from FCA to:

Donna Noonan, Bethany Hermes, Teri Wolfgang,
Ashley Grosse, Jill Ewert and everyone who worked
tirelessly to make this project happen.

To all the athletes and coaches who are:
Sharing Christ boldly;
Seeking Christ passionately;
Leading others faithfully;
and Loving others unconditionally.

To Bill Greig III, Roger Thompson, Steven Lawson, Mark Weising,
Rob Williams and David Griffing at Regal Books.

To all FCA staff across the country who demonstrate
integrity, serving, teamwork and excellence as they work
to see the world impacted for Jesus Christ.

"IMPACTING THE WORLD FOR CHRIST THROUGH SPORTS"

The Fellowship of Christian Athletes is touching millions of lives ... one heart at a time. Since 1954, the Fellowship of Christian Athletes has been challenging coaches and athletes on the professional, college, high school, junior high and youth levels to use the powerful medium of athletics to impact the world for Jesus Christ. FCA is the largest interdenominational, school-based, Christian sports ministry in America. FCA focuses on serving local communities by equipping, empowering and encouraging people to make a difference for Christ.

VISION

To see the world impacted for Jesus Christ
through the influence of athletes and coaches.

MISSION

To present to athletes and coaches and all whom they influence the challenge and adventure of receiving Jesus Christ as Savior and Lord, serving Him in their relationships and in the fellowship of the church.

MINISTRIES

The FCA Ministries encourage, equip and empower coaches and athletes on the professional, college, high school, junior high and youth levels to use the powerful medium of sports to impact their world for Jesus Christ.

The FCA Ministries are:

- **Coaches**
- **Campus**
- **Camp**
- **Community**

FUNDAMENTALS

SHARE Him Boldly
SEEK Him Passionately
LEAD Others Faithfully
LOVE Others Unconditionally

VALUES

Our relationships will demonstrate steadfast commitment to Jesus Christ and His Word through **Integrity, Serving, Teamwork and Excellence**.

Fellowship of Christian Athletes
8701 Leeds Road · Kansas City, MO 64129
www.fca.org · fca@fca.org · 1-800-289-0909

I am a Christian first and last.
I am created in the likeness of God Almighty to bring Him glory.
I am a member of Team Jesus Christ.
I wear the colors of the cross.

I am a Competitor now and forever.
I am made to strive, to strain, to stretch and to succeed in the arena of competition.
I am a Christian Competitor and as such, I face my challenger with the face of Christ.

I do not trust in myself.
I do not boast in my abilities or believe in my own strength.
I rely solely on the power of God.
I compete for the pleasure of my Heavenly Father, the honor
of Christ and the reputation of the Holy Spirit.

My attitude on and off the field is above reproach—my conduct beyond criticism.
Whether I am preparing, practicing or playing,
I submit to God's authority and those He has put over me.
I respect my coaches, officials, teammates, and competitors out of respect for the Lord.

My body is the temple of Jesus Christ.
I protect it from within and without.
Nothing enters my body that does not honor the Living God.
My sweat is an offering to my Master. My soreness is a sacrifice to my Savior.

I give my all—all the time.
I do not give up. I do not give in. I do not give out.
I am the Lord's warrior—a competitor by conviction and a disciple of determination.
I am confident beyond reason because my confidence lies in Christ.
The results of my effort must result in His glory.

Let the competition begin.
Let the glory be God's.

Sign the Creed
Go to www.fca.org

COMPETITORS for CHRIST

THE COACH'S MANDATE

Pray as though nothing of eternal value is going
to happen in my athletes' lives unless God does it.

Prepare each practice and game as giving "my utmost for His highest."

Seek not to be served by my athletes for personal gain, but seek
to serve them as Christ served the church.

Be satisfied not with producing a good record, but with producing good athletes.

Attend carefully to my private and public walk with God, knowing that the
athlete will never rise to a standard higher than that being lived by the coach.

Exalt Christ in my coaching, trusting the Lord will then draw athletes to Himself.

Desire to have a growing hunger for God's Word, for personal
obedience, for fruit of the spirit and for saltiness in competition.

Depend solely upon God for transformation—one athlete at a time.

Preach Christ's word in a Christ-like demeanor, on and off the field of competition.

Recognize that it is impossible to bring glory to both myself
and Christ at the same time.

Allow my coaching to exude the fruit of the Spirit,
thus producing Christ-like athletes.

Trust God to produce in my athletes His chosen purposes,
regardless of whether the wins are readily visible.

Coach with humble gratitude, as one privileged to be God's coach.

FELLOWSHIP OF
CHRISTIAN ATHLETES

COMPETITORS for CHRIST

RESOURCES TO HELP YOUNG ATHLETES

understand how to have the attitude and heart
of a servant, even in the heat of competition.

Revell
a division of Baker Publishing Group
www.RevellBooks.com

Available wherever books and ebooks are sold.

Inspiration and Guidance for a Life of
INTEGRITY and EXCELLENCE

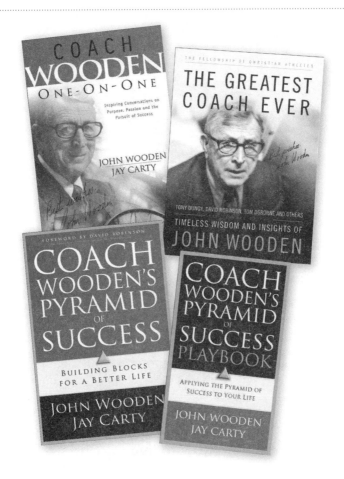

Coach, you can impact every area of your athletes' lives.

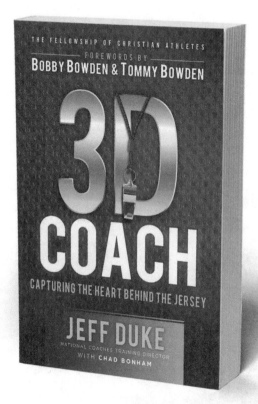

Will you just teach the game or will you teach them how to live for Christ?

Coach Wooden Knew the Long-Term Impact of LITTLE THINGS DONE WELL

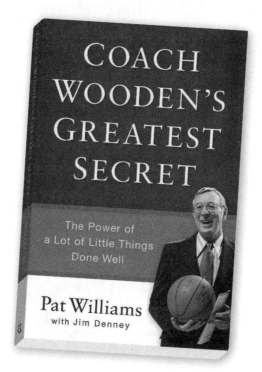

A motivational message filled with life-changing insights and memorable stories—Pat Williams shares why the secret to success in life depends on a lot of little things done well.

Revell
a division of Baker Publishing Group
www.RevellBooks.com

Available wherever books and ebooks are sold.

LEGENDS AREN'T BORN.
They're MADE.

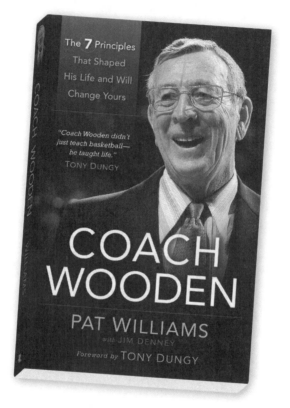

Based on seven principles given to Coach Wooden by his father,
this book helps the reader discover how to be successful and a person
of character and integrity.